The Law of Love

The Law of Love

W Vernon Higham

WVHIGHAMTRUST

THE LAW OF LOVE

WVHIGHAMTRUST
(UK Registered Charity No 1122161)

Website: www.wvhigham.org

UK Registered Office
112 The Philog
Cardiff CF14 1ED

ISBN 978-0-9559637-0-4

Cover design by Andrew Owen.

Printed in Great Britain by Stephens & George, Merthyr Tydfil, UK.

The Law of Love

Contents

Introduction		9
1	Chapter 1	15
2	Chapter 2	27
3	Chapter 3	39
4	Chapter 4	47
5	Chapter 5	57
6	Chapter 6	65
7	Chapter 7	71
8	Chapter 8	79
9	Chapter 9	87
10	Chapter 10	93

Audio sermons of Vernon Higham are available for listening to, or downloading, on the WVHigham Trust website: www.wvhigham.org

Individual CDs and CD boxed sets are also available, and can be ordered by contacting WVHigham Trust: contact@wvhigham.org

Further audio sermons of Vernon Higham are available for listening to, or downloading, on the Tabernacle Cardiff website: www.tabernaclecardiff.org

Information about other titles by Vernon Higham is available through the WVHigham Trust.

"It would be impossible for men and women to fulfil the law of God because of their fallen nature. Nevertheless, it has the important function of being our schoolmaster, to teach us that, despite all our efforts, we fall short of the glory of God. God, in His mercy, has looked upon us and has helped us. He sent His Son into this world to fulfil these laws in our place, and to bear the punishment of our failure in His sacrifice on Calvary. When we, by the grace of God, have come to believe in the Lord Jesus Christ as our Saviour, a new life has begun. The very same law that broke our hearts now becomes the rule of life. Every believer is given grace to enable him to love God and his neighbour, which is something he could not have done before. He is now able to live to the glory of God. The law of God cannot be dismissed, as it is God's will that we should be a holy people and, henceforth, this is our path. **"**

W Vernon Higham

The Law of Love
Introduction

Who is God?

In the Bible, we are told that God is love. This great, holy and mysterious God, who is the key to all existence and the upholder of all that is created, is a God of love. In the pages of Scripture, we learn that the concept of love is a very high one. It is pure and separate from anything that is unworthy or unclean. In the Ten Commandments, the same principle is evident. We can divide the commandments into two groups: the one showing the correct attitude we should have towards God, and the other showing the correct attitude we should have towards one another. In the commandments regarding God Himself, we learn that to love Him with all our being means to honour His person, His name and His day; in the commandments regarding our behaviour towards one another, we learn that loving one another means not doing certain things. We shall call these commandments the *Law of Love* and draw out some glorious positives from these glorious negatives.

What is the Gospel?

In the New Testament, we are introduced to the great Gospel of our God. It is here that we learn of the virgin birth of the Lord Jesus Christ. We are given an account of a life that is without sin and that is well-pleasing in the sight of God. The great purpose of His coming is given to us in all four Gospels in the account of His death on the cross, and His real and physical resurrection. We read of this great purpose in *John 3.16*: 'For God so loved the world, that he gave his only begotten Son, that whosoever believeth in him should not perish, but have everlasting life.' This is the great event that makes the Bible a most meaningful book to us, the one event that really matters in this world, in as far as the salvation of our immortal souls is concerned.

What is Man?

To understand the cross of our Lord Jesus Christ, we must first discover something about ourselves, and until we make this discovery, we shall not see the wonder of the love of God. Sadly, we must learn a painful truth about ourselves: we are sinful. We are vaguely aware of this fact when we grudgingly concede that we are not perfect. In *Romans 3.23*, we read: 'For all have sinned and come short of the glory of God.' It appears to be a cryptic comment, but everything is there. It becomes clear that God has a glory all of His own; it is pure and inaccessible and far beyond the reach of man. Man will always fall short whatever his achievement may be. If we consider the beauty of art in paintings and sculpture, the heights and depths of a myriad of notes in music and the expanse of words in poetry and prose, or man's scientific, technological knowledge and advancement and all his philosophies and ideologies, he falls short! Why? It is because of sin. Man is sinful by nature.

Why is man like this? In the beginning, when this almighty God created the heavens and the earth, He also created man. It was intended that man should have fellowship with God and enjoy the loveliness of God's presence. Satan, the father of lies, however, intervened and tempted the first woman to eat of the fruit that God had forbidden both husband and wife to eat. Eve succumbed to Satan's evil device and, in turn, tempted her husband, Adam, to eat of this fruit. As a result, their innocence disappeared, they became aware of their nakedness and hence hid from the presence of God. This great act of disobedience caused the Fall and all mankind has sprung from its very loins. Man is a sinner because of the Fall. We are sinners by nature.

Can the Gulf be Bridged?

The problem becomes increasingly evident when God is working upon a soul and beckoning it into a relationship with Himself. It is impossible for the gulf between man and God to be bridged by man because of his sin. Furthermore, all his thinking is tainted by sin. It clouds his mind and veils his heart from any true understanding or vision of God.

In the Ten Commandments, God's request is a simple one. He is calling man to live a worthwhile life on earth by loving God with all his heart, soul, and mind, and by loving his neighbour as he loves himself. This is frustratingly impossible for man to achieve because his sinful nature produces a love of self. This means that man lives at a very low level and is forever endeavouring to have, or to do, things that gratify his lusts or his vanity. Sometimes, there have been pathetic efforts by man to justify himself, either by endless religious observances of one kind or another, or by being 'nice'. A so-called 'nice' person believes he is a reasonably good and fair person in his own sight, and probably in the eyes of his friends as well. But, to love God with all his heart and soul and his neighbour as himself, is quite impossible.

When a man's heart is moved by the Spirit of God, there is a great longing, deep in his soul, that cannot be satisfied with anyone or anything other than God. How sad it is that we try so many things which are useless until, at last, we begin to pursue, in earnest, this holy God of love!

It is this consciousness of man's inability to come to God that causes him to grieve over his sinful nature. The longing for God, once begun, cannot easily be silenced. The soul will now find the grace of God truly irresistible. It is then that the spiritual worth of the Gospel becomes evident to the soul of man. A great miracle is taking place that will completely change the whole direction of his life and soul. A spiritual power that comes from the triune God is in action. The Holy Spirit is quickening and awakening his soul and spirit to see his terrible condition and his dreadful destiny. His view of heaven and hell become terribly real and this realisation grips him: that God, alone, can save his soul.

The Unique Person of Christ

In all this, let us consider the Person of the Lord Jesus Christ. Why do we look to Him rather than any other great religious name? It is because He is the only begotten Son of God; in Him, we find true deity and true humanity. The prophets foretold His coming, but the plan was made in eternity. The life of the Lord Jesus Christ so fulfils the requirement of the law of God, that God speaks from heaven and declares Him to be His only begotten Son in whom He is well pleased, and that men should listen to Him. When we come to the cross of our Lord Jesus Christ, the wonder of its meaning slowly dawns upon us: His death was a *violent* one, which helps us to remember the horror of sin in the sight of God; His death was *vicarious,* in that He died in the place of others that they might benefit; His death is *victorious,* in that Satan's plans to spoil the work of God were frustrated.

The death of our Lord Jesus Christ on Calvary was a *complete* work which made it possible for man to come to God. When a man's soul has been so touched by God's mercy, he comes into an everlasting relationship with God. What could be more reassuring than passages of God's Word, such as *Romans 8.35-39?* 'Who shall separate us from the love of Christ? Shall tribulation, or distress, or persecution, or famine, or nakedness, or peril, or sword? As it is written, for Thy sake we are killed all the day long; we are accounted as sheep for the slaughter. Nay, in all these things we are more than conquerors through Him that loved us. For I am persuaded, that neither death, nor life, nor angels, nor principalities, nor powers, nor things present, nor things to come, nor height, nor depth, nor any other creature, shall be able to separate us from the love of God, which is in Christ Jesus our Lord.' The life of the Lord Jesus Christ counts for the believer as having fulfilled the law of God, and His death takes all the guilt and punishment that a man deserves for failing to keep His law.

We must, however, be aware that a man is not automatically received by God the moment he understands the teaching of the Bible. There is an approach to the *mind* where we *understand*; to the *heart* where we *embrace* the truth; and also the *will* where we *commit* ourselves to the redemption that we find in the Lord Jesus Christ.

When we come to the Lord, we have need of repentance and faith. It is God who enables our sorrow to be holy sorrow. It is God's gift when the longing soul receives that faith which leads him to the Lord Jesus Christ. In *Ephesians 2.8*, we read: 'For by grace are ye saved through faith; and that not of yourselves: it is the gift of God.'

A New Sensibility

Man is now in a relationship with God which can never be broken because it rests upon the finished work of Jesus Christ and the promises of God. He also stands in a new position with regard to the law of God. Previously, the law condemned him, as he could in no way fulfil it. However, in the Lord Jesus Christ, he sees the fulfilment of all the law's requirements on his behalf, securing his position before a holy God.

How, then, does the law apply to the believer? It is still God's law and by the grace of God, he is given a new ability both to love and follow the way of obedience. Loving God and his fellow man becomes the pattern for his life. Yet, all is different and new. Whereas before, every effort to obey the law was doomed to miserable failure, now, by God's grace, he is able to live a new life because he is a new creature in Christ. It is important to avoid a legalistic attitude, yet a man of grace finds great delight in obeying God's law. In a world of such sorrow and disorder, here, at last, is order in life.

The law of God is clearly divided into two major parts. In the first part, we are told what it means to love God, and how to approach His person; a right view of God is like a keystone to our Christian life and worship. The other major theme, our attitude toward one another, gives us a realistic view of what it means to love our neighbour. We are now presented with great challenges: to *live for God* in a sinful world; to *triumph over sin*, where once we failed; to *prove the faith* that overcomes wickedness and the evils of our day and world. In the following chapters, we shall proceed, step by step, in the way that He has commanded that we should walk.

The Law of Love

Chapter One

Thou shalt have no other gods before me.
Exodus 20.3

What have the Ten Commandments to do with a Christian? Can we not be lawless? Can we not be licentious in our living? Can we not now neglect the Sabbath and do as we like? Need we bow to the authority of God in any way, to His Word or to the pattern of the church, the pastor and the elders? Need we take any notice? Are these things important at all? Very often, a Christian is puzzled. There are many who have a wrong view of the law of God. It is true that the law of God measures us and shows us that we have fallen short of the glory of God. It is true that the law of God condemns us. Yet the law of God is from God Himself; it is holy and pure. It is His demand. He wants us to love Him and Him alone. We *must* love God.

The aim of the law is to make us holy in our behaviour and holy in our lives. This is why it is dangerous when we have forms of evangelicalism that ignore any kind of holiness of life. It is equally dangerous to have a legalism that ignores the joy of the Lord. The Bible is quite clear about it: the aim of the law is that we might be a holy people. God is saying to believers, 'If I come into your heart, I come to rule and to reign. I come there to sit on the throne. I will have no other gods; I will have none other that will take away your affection. I will have *all* your affection. I will have *all* your love. I must reign.'

If we break these commandments, it is important to remember that we are answerable, not in the day of judgement, but in the day of Christ *(2 Corinthians 5.10)*. We might ask, 'Are we still under the law?' No, we are not under the law, yet we must look at the law. The Ten Commandments are commandments of love although they do not actually talk about love. Very often, you will hear people saying, 'I love God, I love Jesus Christ, I love this, I love that,' and there is no content to the word 'love'. It is just a word, a sound, with no substance to it. It is the Lord Jesus Christ who shows us that the heart of the law is to love God and to love one another. He plainly states, in *Matthew 5.17*: 'Think not that I am come to destroy the law, or the prophets: I am not come to destroy, but to fulfil.'

The Lord Jesus Christ has in mind a standard of love, righteousness and goodness far above the religion of the Jews at the time. In *Matthew 5.20*, He goes on to say: 'For I say unto you, that except your righteousness shall exceed the righteousness of the scribes and Pharisees, ye shall in no case enter into the kingdom of heaven.' The Pharisees could keep a law and break it simultaneously; they had a legalistic way of saying they kept the law, and a clever way of breaking it. God says that He wants us to understand the law and He wants us to be able to have the grace to fulfil the law.

It is the law of love. Let us examine it: its *depth* reaches our deepest, dirtiest, vilest sin and forbids it absolutely; its *height* reaches the perfection of the pure worship of God, the absolute love of God; its *breadth* embraces my meanest enemy, and forgives; its *length* is from the day we are born to the day that we die; its demands are perfection. This law is far reaching in its effects; it removes the love of sin and replaces it with the love of all that is right, and the love of God. This is the law of love.

Christ, Our Fulfilment

We must remember that we are thinking of the Christian. He has already learnt that he is unable to keep these laws and has come to the place where he seeks the hand of God. In the Lord Jesus Christ, we find our fulfilment: in His death as a penalty for our failure, and in His life as a glorious fulfilment of the requirements of God. When a man stands as one who trusts entirely upon the grace of God through the Lord Jesus Christ, he finds that he has a living faith which leads him in a better way. The Jew could not hope to fulfil the law; not even the Pharisees could hope to fulfil it. No man can fulfil this law on his own; it is beyond his capabilities. Yet, in Christ, grace is given that enables the Christian to follow this way. He is then able to love God, as we read in *1 John 4.19*: 'We love him, because he first loved us.' It is in this way that we are able to have a righteousness which exceeds that of the Pharisees.

Christ is the fulfilment of the law. He fulfils the requirements of the law of God in His life, by loving God with all His soul, all His heart and all His being and by loving His neighbour as Himself. Christ receives the penalty of the law; He takes upon Himself the sinner's iniquity and lawlessness, and nails it to the cross at Calvary. He gives us His righteousness. As Robert Murray M'Cheyne says in his well-loved hymn: '*Dressed in beauty not my own.*' God the Father looks on us as found in Him.

Can we say that the law is then finished? 'God forbid!' says Paul. The Lord Jesus Christ did all that He did for us in order that He might live in our lives and give us grace that we might be able to fulfil that law. *Romans 7.22* is written from a believer's standpoint: 'For I delight in the law of God after the inward man.' We are now able to say that Christ died and paid the penalty for our sins, yet as believers with new ability, new grace and new resources, we will delight to do His law. What has happened? He has changed us and has taken us in His hands and remade us. We are now new creatures, as *Ephesians 2.10* tells us: 'For we are his workmanship, created in Christ Jesus unto good works which God hath before ordained that we should walk in them.' The very law that condemned us now becomes the rule of our lives.

Where does love come into this? If we want to love God, the nature of this love must be spelled out. The Ten Commandments declare the two things that are expected of the Christian – to love God and to love our fellow man. But, we look at them through the spectacles of the New Testament, with the eyes of grace and the eyes of a ransomed sinner. In our hearts, there is now a burning desire to fulfil the law of God. It will not save us. Christ has saved us, and we long to fulfil His law by God's grace alone, for which we are answerable in the day of Christ.

(1) The Person of God

To love God, first and foremost, means this: 'Thou shall have no other gods before me'. God is telling us that no one else, or indeed nothing else, must take His place. In truth, there are no other gods, but men always make their own gods, whether they are man-made idols representing false deities, or men who have elevated themselves to a God-like status, or the mundane things that surround us, which take our supreme attention – attention and devotion that should be directed towards the only God.

What is God like? Men have strange ideas of God, and build up a character of their own imagination which has no resemblance to the God of the Scriptures. God, the Father of our Lord Jesus Christ, is clearly and accurately presented to us in the books of the Bible. He is consistent in all that He is. When we are commending this character of God, we must remember that we are not describing an ordinary person. He is the Lord of all creation. There are some qualities which belong to Him that could never be shared by us. They belong to God because He is God. We call these His incommunicable attributes. Then, there are other attributes or qualities which we call His communicable attributes. But, even then, we can only share in a shadow of them, as they are bound to be expressed perfectly only in our God.

Let us consider a few of those things that convey the nature of God. He is almighty: He is *omnipotent*. There is no one who can ever come near to the might of His strength. No creature is able to compare with His ability and power. If we are afraid of the ideologies that threaten today, they are nothing. If we are afraid of the circumstances that may come upon us, they are nothing. He is almighty.

God is everywhere: He is *omnipresent*. At first, this seems a strange thought to us, but if we begin to limit Him to one place, we realise that it cannot be. He must have this ability of being everywhere. In a way, it seems beyond our understanding, and yet, it is so right. No power is beyond Him; nothing is too difficult for Him in this world. We do not have to wait to get a message to Him, wondering how long it will take. Even when we are desperate at times to make contact with someone by phone, for example, in a hospital, the line can be busy. Not so when approaching the throne of grace: we have full and immediate access to our God because He is omnipresent.

He knows everything: He is *omniscient*. What a relief! Deep down in our hearts, we would not have it otherwise. He knows exactly what He is dealing with when He is dealing with us. He knows every particle of dust. He knows every shade of anxiety in our hearts. He knows the anguish. He knows the joy. He knows the secret motives. He knows our cunning. He knows our kindnesses. He knows all. This knowledge amazed both Nathanael, when the Lord told him that He had seen him under the fig tree before he approached, and the woman of Samaria when the Lord told her that He knew her past.

He is *eternal*, outside and above time, in a dimension of reality that leaves our minds failing, and yet we know that it must be. He is *infinite*: He is without limit. We cannot contain God in that we can say, 'all of God can be contained.' There is no end to the knowing of God. He is *sovereign*: He is supreme over every conceivable thing and situation and reigns in timeless majesty over all.

Then, God can be described with qualities that can be ours when we are Christians. He has all these, in perfection. He desires that His people should be righteous, holy, good and loving. When we say that God is *righteous*, we are considering the absolute heart of righteousness. In all His actions, God is right, because He chooses to be so. God is *holy*, and His holiness of character is described as pure, burning light. We have an image of intense heat or intense cold, but with either, it is a burning pure heat or cold, intense in its great influence and power of purity. He is holy. There are no devious dealings with God or by Him. He is clean, possessing nothing dirty. God is *good*. The Lord Jesus Christ described His Father as good, in such a way as to make the concept very special. The powerful knowledge that God is not bad, but that He is positively good, encourages us. Lastly, can we ever forget that God is *love*? He is love, and yet there is more. That is only the fringe. There are many ways of describing the attributes of God. Even if we took a most complicated attribute and then enlarged upon it, there is more and more! More than even our enlightened understanding can take in here on earth! There is always more. This is God, and He is our God. The greatest fulfilment that there can ever be for a man is to discover what it means to worship Him. This worshipping heart is captured in the lines of a hymn by Oliver Wendell Holmes:

> *Lord of all being, throned afar,*
> *Thy glory flames from sun and star;*
> *Centre and soul of every sphere,*
> *Yet to each loving heart how near.*

> *Our midnight is Thy smile withdrawn;*
> *Our noontide is Thy gracious dawn;*
> *Our rainbow arch, Thy mercy's sign;*
> *All, save the clouds of sin, are Thine*

We must begin our Christian life by understanding this first commandment. Perhaps when we have begun to understand the character of God, we will realize that it must be so. These attributes weave their way through the pages of Scripture and, by grace, we come to know Him and adore His majestic person.

(2) The Place of God

From this commandment, we learn that there is but one place for God in our lives, and that is on the throne of our hearts, ruling as Saviour and Lord. It is hardly right or reasonable to offer any other place than the throne, or offer Him any less than our total allegiance. It is in the light and knowledge of His greatness that we realise that His place must be foremost. Nevertheless, it often takes some time for us to realise and recognise this, and then to act upon it. We cannot say, 'I would like You, Lord, to be in my life; I have here a little three-cornered stool – perhaps You would like to sit here?' or 'I have a spare dining chair.' No! He must have the throne: He comes to reign and to rule. He assures us that if we want to learn to love Him, He will teach us, and if we want to love Him, we must understand who He is. In a world that is totally opposed in its philosophy of life and its preoccupation with self-gratification, it seems almost a remote cry to respond to the plea of this holy God. Yet, this world, with all its busyness, will eventually pass away, and the silence of eternity awaits. God is always there; there is nowhere in creation where we can escape Him. Slowly, we begin to realise that the last and absolutely final word on everything is God's. That being so, and knowing that we are without excuse, we must be doers of His Word and will, as well as hearers.

How can we give God His rightful place? We know that, of ourselves, we are unable to love. We do not possess the quality of love that will enable us to love God as we ought. Indeed, we are God haters by nature, hateful and hating one another. We even love darkness more than light. How, therefore, can we love Him? We are able to love Him through Christ. The path to loving Him is through the path of pardon, as expressed in this translation of William Williams' hymn:

> There is a path of pardon
>   In His blood;
> There is a sure salvation
>   In His blood.
> The law's full consummation,
> A Father's approbation –
> Hear Zion's acclamation!
>   In His blood –
> Atonement and redemption
>   In His blood!

Why does He have to be on the throne of our lives? He reminds us: 'Lest we forget Gethsemane, lest we forget Thine agony.' He bids us look at His Son, look at His blood, look at what He has done and see what we have in Him. Can we refuse the throne for such love?

We must, then, consider how this affects our daily lives. We begin with ourselves and examine our attitudes, our motives and our affections. Let us make sure that the Lord reigns there. It is so easy to decide on a certain course of action because it is the most suitable and convenient way. It is true, however, that we must play our part because we find that the Scriptures lay down very clear principles and laws for us to work out and to follow, as we are told in Philippians 2.12-13: 'Work out your own salvation with fear and trembling. For it is God which worketh in you both to will and to do of his good pleasure.'

What is the cost of such love? A great responsibility is laid upon us to work out all the implications of our actions in our lives and their effect upon others. Nevertheless, an obedient spirit that is willing to work things out, is immediately given grace to see through every situation.

In our family relationships, there is a sensitive area where we must be very conscious of honouring our parents, yet no one must come before God in our hearts. The Lord Jesus Christ expressed it in very definite terms, as it is recorded in *Luke 14.26*: 'If any man come to me, and hate not his father, and mother, and wife, and children, and brethren, and sisters, yea, and his own life also, he cannot be my disciple.' Even if it is our father or our mother, our son or our daughter, our dearest friend, or anyone, that is driving God from our breast, then we must mourn that it is so. A state of enmity is created; they come between us and God. *Nothing* must come between us and God. For a moment, we are not to worry about our father and our mother, or our brother or our sister. We must get our priorities right. We must look at Calvary.

The strange thing is this, that the person who loves God more than all, loves his relatives and friends far better than the man who does not love God. Once we tear ourselves away from putting them first and put God first, we are able to love them better than we ever loved before. We love them better than those who cling to their loved ones and who do not believe in God. Wherever we are, the same principle holds: God first, simply because He is God, and worthy of our undivided affection. The hymn writer Jenny Evelyn Hussey recognised this principle in her life when she penned these words:

> *King of my life, I crown Thee now,*
> *Thine shall the glory be;*
> *Lest I forget Thy thorn-crowned brow,*
> *Lead me to Calvary.*

(3) The Peace of God

Many people will say that it must be a burden to be a Christian. To them, we seem deprived of worldly enjoyment, and must, of necessity, be most miserable. In *Matthew 11.29-30*, we read that the Lord Jesus

Christ said: 'Take my yoke upon you, and learn of me; for I am meek and lowly in heart: and ye shall find rest unto your souls. For my yoke is easy, and my burden is light.' There is a peace in the relationship of grace which is very special: to know that our sins are forgiven and that the enmity between God and ourselves is removed forever. There is peace for the Christian in the law of God as it is now planted and written in his heart. *Psalm 119.165* speaks of this peace: 'Great peace have they which love thy law: and nothing shall offend them.'

How do we let Him reign in our hearts? *Colossians 3.15* says: 'And let the peace of God rule in your hearts.' It does not say, 'Let the peace of God have a say in your lives.' It does not say, 'Let the peace of God rule on the border of your lives.' No! The text says, 'Let the peace of God *rule* in your hearts.' In the parallel passage in the epistle to the *Philippians*, we are told that the peace of God shall keep our hearts and minds through Christ Jesus *(Philippians 4.7)*. It works both ways: the peace of God keeps us, and those who love God's law have perfect peace.

We must consider that we are living in troubled times, when there is no peace between the nations and a restless spirit is at work. The terrible repercussions of this restlessness are manifested in unhappy employer-employee relationships, unhappy homes, and a generation of lost individuals. The whole purpose of life seems to have gone astray and a very frightened world is terrified of what tomorrow holds. This is not true of the Christian, who, realising the present situation, puts his trust in God. He knows that, because God is first in his heart, he is precious in the sight of God. This makes an amazing difference to the present and to the future, the known and the unknown.

Another Dimension

The Christian's life is orientated around God and this gives another dimension to the understanding of life. The secret is to honour God and give Him the place that is due to Him. God will lose none of our love. Imagine our hearts as if they were containers; we pour out all our love at the throne but keep just one drop back. 'Just a moment,' God says, 'where are you taking that? Come back here.' As Thomas Watson puts it in *The Ten Commandments*, 'Love is the soul of religion and that which constitutes a real Christian. Love is the queen of graces; it shines and sparkles in God's eye.'

To know is one thing; to do, another. But, in obedience to that which we know, there is great peace. We are promised that, whatever may be ours, when we love His law, nothing shall offend us in life. How can we love Thee, Lord? Teach us lesson number one: 'Thou shall have no other gods before me.'

The Law of Love

Chapter Two

Thou shalt not make unto thee any graven image.
Exodus 20.4

Thou shalt not make unto thee any graven image, or any likeness of any thing that is in heaven above, or that is in the earth beneath, or that is in the water under the earth: thou shalt not bow down thyself to them, nor serve them: for I the Lord thy God am a jealous God, visiting the iniquity of the fathers upon the children unto the third and fourth generation of them that hate me; and shewing mercy unto thousands of them that love me, and keep my commandments *(Exodus 20.4-6)*.

In the first commandment, we are told to put God first, and the second follows hard after this and fully confirms the statement. Nothing is worthy of our worship other than God. The solemnity of this is emphasised by the severity of the presentation, stating that God's sure displeasure can follow us for many generations if we dare to disobey.

It is important to remind ourselves that we are speaking from the Christian point of view, a person standing in the grace of God. No longer do we fear the condemnation of God because the Lord Jesus

Christ has met all the requirements of God on our behalf. Toplady understood this very well when he penned these lines:

> *The terrors of law and of God*
> *With me can have nothing to do;*
> *My Saviour's obedience and blood*
> *Hide all my transgressions from view.*

Freedom or Licence

The Christian is a free person. *John 8.36* tells us: 'If the Son therefore shall make you free, ye shall be free indeed.' Sadly, however, this word 'freedom' is misunderstood in our present generation. We were once in bondage, and in the captivity of Satan, as the hymn writer Charles Wesley puts it, *'fast bound in sin and nature's night'*. Once we are in Christ, however, we are no longer in this bondage, but free; free to do something that we could not do before, and that is to love God and to love our neighbour. Previously, our captive hearts could only love ourselves. We were incapable of loving God with all our heart, soul and mind. Sometimes, we were capable of a little expression of devotion but we did everything to gratify ourselves.

This freedom has often been interpreted as a freedom to live as we like, and to sin. The apostle Paul, in *Romans 6.2*, writes: 'God forbid. How shall we, that are dead to sin, live any longer therein?'

As an illustration, let us consider a child randomly playing on the keys of a piano. In a way, we could call it freedom. It is a freedom that we would soon tire of, if we knew anything about basic melody or the rules of music. This is not freedom, but licence! If we, then, consider the child being taken in hand by the teacher and taught something of the rigours of the discipline of music, then that child would begin to produce something new. Before long, he leaves the so-called freedom of expression on the piano, and, at long last, a recognisable tune emerges. Should the child be gifted with genius, his newfound freedom would give a flood of expression as his fingers danced along the keys. There is, however, a difference: there is order and melody. Similarly, when we are free to love God, there is the order and melody of grace in our lives.

The law of God becomes the means of a wonderful expression of love and is acceptable in the sight of God. Grace has made this possible, and a life of obedience comes into fruition. In this second commandment, we begin to learn something of God as a character. He is not a set of remote, albeit perfect, principles, but a living, vital being. He is jealous of our love and would have none of it wasted upon some lesser thing.

(1) The Authority of God

There is a very powerful note of authority in this commandment which forbids us to make any graven image or likeness to God. So prone is man towards the idolatrous, in some form or another, that he is clearly warned against this degenerate form of worship. Even in his spiritual activity with God Himself, there must be nothing of the savour of idolatry brought into the worship. It must be pure and clean. Idols can even creep into Christianity; from the worship of idols to making an idol of a person or thing, they all stand condemned in the sight of God. No one, nothing, must stand between our hearts and Himself in both our relationship and our worship. In no way must we waste our love and our worship upon these lesser things. We are exhorted thus in *Exodus 20.5*: 'Thou shalt not bow down thyself to them, nor serve them: for I the Lord thy God am a jealous God.'

When we speak of jealousy in one another, it is an unpleasant thing and savours of selfishness and possessiveness, but when we refer to the jealousy of God, it is very different. In His sight, a great price has been paid for us and we are not our own. The apostle Paul reminds us of this in *1 Corinthians 6.19-20*: 'What? know ye not that your body is the temple of the Holy Ghost which is in you, which ye have of God, and ye are not your own? For ye are bought with a price: therefore glorify

God in your body, and in your spirit, which are God's.'

It is a painful thing for Him to watch this costly possession giving its love, time and service to that which is impure, when His pure love is ours and awaits us. He is jealous for our good and, therefore, totally unwilling that there should be a sinful waste in the lives of His children. We must endeavour to capture this truth more and more. Such love demands our soul, our life, our heart, our all. He owns us. We belong to Him. How can we live for Him? He gives us grace to do so. If we find difficulties, if we find self-love intruding, if we find the flesh with all its desires trying to battle against the new creature in Christ, what then? Remember Calvary. In *Romans 8.32*, we are reminded again that God freely gave His only Son, Jesus Christ, for us: 'He that spared not his own Son, but delivered him up for us all, how shall he not with him also freely give us all things?'

If ever our love for God fades, remember how the Lord Jesus Christ fulfilled the law of God in His life; remember how He took the penalty of our failure on Calvary; remember the quality of the love of God, and how this love has been given to the utmost. He cares for us; He cares for our every anxiety, our every worry. He cares for us so much that He has given His Son and we belong to Him. We sing of this love in Charles Wesley's great hymn:

> *Love divine, all loves excelling,*
> *Joy of heaven, to earth come down,*
> *Fix in us Thy humble dwelling,*
> *All Thy faithful mercies crown.*

In the light of such love, there is a rightness in the pure and holy jealousy of God. It is no small matter to Him whom we love and serve, and it should be no small matter to us to heed His note of authority.

In the Scriptures, marriage between a man and a woman is compared to the union between Christ and the Church. In the marriage vows, we are told, 'and keep thyself only unto him'. If we lift these words to the arrangement of the covenant we have with God, we see that God keeps Himself for us, and He expects us to keep ourselves for Him. Let us look to Him and heed His voice, for He is God. We must earnestly desire to emulate William Cowper's prayer:

> *The dearest idol I have known,*
> *Whate'er that idol be,*
> *Help me to tear it from Thy throne,*
> *And worship only Thee.*

(2) The Attitude of God.

We learn from God's second commandment that God will also preserve His will amongst His people. We must remember that we have received great mercy at the hand of God. We are now His people; we have an inheritance, and this great privilege should never be taken lightly. There is nothing light-hearted about the Gospel at all. Most certainly it produces joy, but it is the clean joy of the sheer delight of belonging to God.

God's words in *Exodus 20.5-6* are solemn and salutary and we need to pause and give them our consideration: '…visiting the iniquity of the fathers upon the children unto the third and fourth generation of them that hate me; and shewing mercy unto thousands of them that love me, and keep my commandments.'

We must be so careful, and even now, consider future generations. A stubborn stance taken on some issue in spiritual matters may gratify pride, but its repercussions can be endless. Somehow, we must capture a view of the positive greatness of God and gladly humble ourselves under His mighty hand. In everything, we must keep in view our love for Him in the keeping of the commandments. How easily we lose sight of our need to love God with all our strength! How easily the world entices us away, and tarnishes and clouds that wonderful relationship of love! We should consider these things carefully.

The complaint against the church at Ephesus in the book of *Revelation* gives a warning to all our hearts: the loss of our first love. How frighteningly true this can be, but how horrifying it is in the sight of God! This was the church that was doctrinally correct, that laboured for the Gospel, that had known persecution and from which many martyrs had arisen. This was also a church with which God was very displeased. This church is clearly described in *Revelation 2.2-3*: 'I know thy works, and thy labour, and thy patience, and how thou canst not bear them which are evil: and thou hast tried them which say they are apostles, and are not, and hast found them liars: and hast borne, and hast patience, and for my name's sake hast laboured, and hast not fainted.'

We might think, 'What a tremendous church!' If any error came, they sorted it out. They persevered in times of adversity. In times of persecution, they even had their own roll of martyrs and, added to this, they did it all, not for their own glory, but for His name's sake. 'But,' says God, 'I have one thing against thee' *(Revelation 2.4)*. Yes, they were doctrinally sound, they made any sacrifice of time or money, and they were even willing to have their bodies burned. Is it possible to do any more than that? Yes, we can hold back that one thing that God requires: our love for Him. If we do not possess this, all that we do is nothing. It will not matter if we say, 'But Lord, I know all about Thy person.' He will answer, 'Do you *love* me?' 'Lord, I know the confession of faith from beginning to end.' He will answer, 'Do you *love* me?' 'Lord, I have laboured and will do many things for Thee.' He will answer, 'Do you *love* me?' 'Lord, I am in the ranks of the martyrs and about to be shot.' He will answer, 'Do you *love* me?' This is the question that we must answer, both as individuals, and as a people of God.

We can find ourselves defending the truths in all the range of the full counsel of God, persevering in the path of faith and all its requirements, and even loyal to the degree of standing in persecution, and yet to have lost something. To lose our love is inexcusable, because it is the heart of the law and the heart of the Gospel. Let us not deceive ourselves: God knows why our hearts have grown cold. Deep in our hearts, we know when things are not as they should be. What, then, shall we do? We must do as the church in Ephesus was exhorted to do, in *Revelation 2.5*: 'Remember therefore from whence thou art fallen, and repent, and do the first works; or else I will come unto thee quickly, and will remove thy candlestick out of his place, except thou repent.'

It is terrible when we begin to notice that we have lost our lustre, and this painful, yet expressive verse by William Cowper becomes a real part of our experience:

> *Where is the blessedness I knew*
> *When first I saw the Lord?*
> *Where is the soul-refreshing view*
> *Of Jesus and His Word?*

What happens to a church that loses its love? God says that He will take its candlestick away. Do we know what He is saying? He is saying that He will withdraw from His people, perhaps for one generation or two, or more; a day and a thousand years are no different to Him. This does not mean that He will not have mercy on individuals. The Gospel has not yet been withdrawn, but look at our churches! They are cold and indifferent. Why has it been so many years since there has been a revival in our land? He has withdrawn. Why is there spiritual declension in Britain today? He has withdrawn.

How do we bring Him back? We need to repent! We have not loved Him as we should. We have neglected Him. We have not put Him on the throne of our church and He has withdrawn. He has the right to do so, because He is God. He can do so for a long, long time, as we see from the example of Samson in the Old Testament who was greatly blessed of God and then he sinned. Somebody else came on to the throne in his life – a woman. Then we read the sad testimony found in

Judges 16 when Samson was oblivious to the withdrawal of God: 'And he wist not that the Lord was departed from him' *(Judges 16.20)*.

Everybody else could see it. He was still the Lord's, but his radiance had gone. The glory and loveliness of God had departed. There he was, strutting around, saying, 'I know the truth, I know God. I am an Israelite. I'm marching to Zion the beautiful city of God.' But, 'he wist not that the Lord was departed from him.' Samson had forgotten what it meant to love God and to make Him his first love. Has that happened to us? We will still go to heaven, but God can withdraw from our lives for decades.

In the *Song of Solomon*, the beloved was lying on her couch and she could hear the latch going. It was her lover. After a while, she very carelessly went to the door. He was always there and she took him for granted. When she eventually opened the door, he had gone. Then she realised how much he meant to her and rushed about the city saying, 'Has anyone seen my lover?' 'What is he like?' she was asked. 'He is fair, he is handsome, he is the Rose of Sharon and the Lily of the Valley. He is the fairest of ten thousand to my soul. He is my bright and Morning Star and he has *withdrawn*...' The people said to her, 'Tell us, if there is such a lover as handsome as that, where we might find him, that we might know him too!' She could not be bothered with their iniquitous and carnal way of thinking. It was so terrible to her that her lover had withdrawn. She cried out and she repented, and then her lover returned. However, first she had to see that she could not play about with the lover of her soul. Similarly, we must not play about with God; we must not lose our first love. He must always be on the throne.

It is necessary to remember God's displeasure. Happily, in Christ, we know that our eternal future is secure. Nevertheless, we must not forget that we will have to stand before Him one day, as we read in *2 Corinthians 5.10*: 'For we must all appear before the judgement seat of Christ.' This serves both as a warning to the Christian to keep on the narrow way and as an incentive to do God's will. There are rewards and punishments, which are quite apart from our salvation.

(3) The Adoration of God

If then we are so solemnly warned about the danger of idol worship, and of following, loving and serving that which is lesser than God, let us consider the implications of loving such a God. Very often we hear the word 'Puritan' treated with dislike and fear, yet the heart of this word contains the word 'pure'. Our worship, in all its expression, is to be pure, so that we might prefer to please God rather than to please men, and so that we might do that which is right rather than that which we want to do. The Lord Jesus Christ was very gracious in His dealings with the woman of Samaria. As He spoke to her, the matter of worship was approached. Let us stay upon this most searching statement made by the Lord Jesus Christ, as we read it in *John 4.23-24*: 'But the hour cometh, and now is, when the true worshippers shall worship the Father in spirit and in truth: for the Father seeketh such to worship him. God is a Spirit: and they that worship him must worship him in spirit and in truth.' Remember that we should have emerged from the shadows of external worship in the Old Testament, which required so many material and physical aids, to the spiritual where we have learnt to mortify the flesh. In the light of all this, the words of the Lord Jesus Christ enter into the centre of what it means to worship God with a heart of love. God is a Spirit, so how shall we worship Him? In spirit and in truth.

Where Does Worship Begin?

The Christian man is in a new position: he is a child of God. A radical change has taken place so that the whole orientation of his life has changed from being man-centred, to being God-centred. We are reminded of this truth by the apostle Paul in *Colossians 3.10*: 'And have put on the new man, which is renewed in knowledge after the image of him that created him.' Man was created in the image of God, but we are not talking about arms and legs. The image we are talking about is that which is mentioned in *Ephesians 4.24*: 'And that ye put on the new man, which after God is created in righteousness and true holiness.'

The image of God that concerns us here is the image of righteousness and holiness. When we become Christians, this image is restored and we become new men. There will come a day when, 'this corruptible shall have put on incorruption' and when, 'this mortal shall have put on immortality' *(1 Corinthians 15.54)*.

The Wrong Way To Worship

Our Lord exalted the body, and one day we shall have a new body, but in our worship, we must *always* keep bodily expression under control. We must never worship like the prophets of Baal. *Never!* Yet, there must be a human expression of worship. Satan will do all he can to lead us along a carnal path. We must keep to the path that is outlined for us in the second commandment: 'Thou shalt not make unto thee any graven image, or any likeness of any thing that is in heaven above, or that is in the earth beneath, or that is in the water under the earth' *(Exodus 20.4)*.

In the early church, there was a big row and the church divided into two: the one became the Greek Orthodox Church and the other the Roman Catholic Church. They split on many points, but there is one point here of interest. The Eastern church (Greek Orthodox) said that the Western church (Roman Catholic) had graven images in their churches. The Eastern church said that there should not be idols but that icons (pictures etc.) were allowed. Man always wants something to look upon, that he might kneel before it. We should understand that it is an insult to God to compare Him with anything on earth because God is a Spirit. The principle ought to be this: sculptor, hold back your chisel when it comes to God the Father, Son and Holy Spirit; painter, hold back your brush when it comes to God the Father, Son and Holy Spirit; actor, hold back your body when it comes to God the Father, Son and Holy Spirit. Otherwise, you blaspheme. We should respect the second commandment which says: 'Thou shalt not make unto thee any graven image' and that is that.

The Correct Way To Worship

There must be an expression of worship. We have a body and we can only express ourselves through our bodies. The body should then respect the reverence and honour that belongs to the Gospel which resides within our hearts. How then can we do this? We must use our voices in as far as it is dignified, disciplined and honouring to God. The preacher must distinguish between that thin line of preaching the truth with his voice, and making an exhibition of himself. In singing, we must watch that thin line between the worship of God and entertainment. It is a line that we are personally responsible for in the day of Christ.

We must preach and we must worship Him in spirit and in truth. We must also express our adoration. We must ask of everything, 'Is this carnal? Is this of the flesh? Is the spirit of the world in this?' God is seeking for believers who will understand what it is to worship Him biblically and correctly. We often hear people saying, 'But we have got to get through to people.' My friends, what is needed is that God might get through to us!

But how carnal we are! When will our little hearts be taken up with God? However can we learn? We must be willing to put ourselves under the discipline of God and His Word. We must honour the truth of the Scriptures and embrace them with our mind, heart and will. To love God means to honour Him as the one, true and living God and to worship Him as such. Our worship of God must be in the power of the Holy Spirit, and our own spirit must be deeply affected by this holy exercise. Our total being, to its very depth, which has been enlightened by God's grace, reaches out to worship the Creator. This must be in spirit and in truth. It speaks of a spiritual intimacy that simply forbids any sign of carnality. Our Lord God is holy and must be worshipped as such. How beautiful true worship is! It fills the heart with godly delight. Monsell's well-loved hymn provides us with a perfect example of true worship:

> *O worship the Lord in the beauty of holiness;*
> *Bow down before Him, His glory proclaim;*
> *With gold of obedience and incense of lowliness,*
> *Kneel and adore Him, the Lord is His Name.*

The Law of Love

Chapter Three

Thou shalt not take
the name of the Lord
thy God in vain.
Exodus 20.7

Thou shalt not take the name of the Lord thy God in vain; for the Lord will not hold him guiltless that taketh his name in vain *(Exodus 20.7)*.

The Lord with whom we are involved and with whom we have to do, is a person, a character, and has a name. In the third commandment, this name is presented to us as one to be respected because it is the name of God. To a Christian, the name of God is especially precious because he is now in a relationship, through God's grace, that can never be severed. It is a name that gladdens our hearts and evokes the most profound respect within us, because it is the name of God. Unbelievers carelessly abuse the name of God in their ignorance, but they do a grievous thing and will not be without guilt in this matter. A Christian must be particularly sensitive, as it is the name of his God. It is so easy for us as believers, in our familiarity, to sin in a subtle way. We must be careful in the way that we think of God, how we address God in our prayers, how we worship Him and how we speak about Him to others. In no way may we take His name in vain, certainly not by blaspheming; but also we must ensure that we do not use His name carelessly, always remembering that He is our God.

The law of God still applies to the Christian, but it is altogether in another dimension. The grace of God has dealt with his heart and his relationship with God is right. This being so, he is directly instructed to be very careful about the name of the Lord. This refers to the Godhead: Father, Son and Holy Spirit. Included, then, should be a profound respect and sense of reverence in the heart of the believer. He has every reason to both revere and love the name of God.

How does the Christian come to revere and love the name of God? The sinner comes to know God as his Father through the work of the Holy Spirit enlightening him and convicting him of his great need. It is in the merits of the Son of God, the Lord Jesus Christ, that he comes to a place where he may receive the forgiveness of his sins and everlasting life. To the Christian, the name of the Lord Jesus Christ is the great entry into the name of God. For these reasons, both the names of Christ and God are precious and revered.

In a day of gross blasphemy, when no respect is shown even to heads of state, we need to consider this commandment with great seriousness. An important part of this reverence and love of God's name is demonstrated in the correct form of worship, where we desire to worship Him in spirit and in truth. In *John 16.14*, the Lord Jesus Christ promised that the Holy Spirit would come to the church which would glorify Him: 'He shall glorify me: for he shall receive of mine, and shall shew it unto you.'

(1) His Name and His Person

The name of God was treated with special reverence amongst the Jews. Indeed, it was so holy that it was not to be uttered. They were allowed to call Him 'Lord', but His name 'Jehovah' (or 'Yahweh' as most scholars think it was pronounced) had to be treated with extreme reverence. We learn from this that His name was not to be taken lightly. Blasphemy to the Jew was a terrible thing, and the severe warnings of God were enough for him.

When we consider the way the name of the Lord Jesus Christ is abused today, it is a very grievous thing to the heart of the Christian, and very hard to bear. The days that we live in are so wicked that men will even go out of their way to blaspheme if they know there is a Christian nearby. Gone, at present, are the days when men would stop swearing and blaspheming in the company of Christians. Their respect towards God is non-existent.

How does this apply to the believer? We are not likely to blaspheme the name of God, but we should not take His name lightly. We have all come across people who are so free with the words 'darling' and 'dear' and 'lovely', yet there is nothing in their lives to show that there is much love. As believers, we can so easily say, 'the Lord told me to do this, the Lord told me to do that...' We must be sure how we are using the name of the Lord and we must treat Him with reverence. There is a great difference between a glib reference to God over every trivial matter, and the sweet mention of His name upon our lips, knowing that He is the Person to whom we take everything in prayer. In every way, we must encourage close fellowship and walking with the Lord, and the happy, yet respectful, use of His name. Let us, once again, come to the place of a personal relationship with God through our Lord Jesus Christ, which allows us to call Him Father and yet maintains the profound relationship of the King and His subject.

It is helpful in this context to study the phrase 'Hallowed be thy name' from the Lord's Prayer. There are three things that the word 'hallowed' includes:

(1) Honour: we are familiar with Him, but there should be no familiarity, no kind of cheekiness. He is our friend; He is our Lord and Master and we are not to be careless in our attitude towards Him. We are to ascribe honour to God and to His name. Our lips should always speak His name with the greatest respect.

(2) Adoration: where shall we adore Him? In our hearts. If we sing *'Jesus*

the Name high over all', our lips will honour Him, but adoration will be in our hearts.

(3) Obedience: what about our lives? What about our arms and legs and bodies? They must be controlled by obedience, so that in our bodies and in our living, all we do should be for His name's sake. All this is included in this word 'hallowed'.

(2) His Name and His Presence

Why is it so wrong to take His name in vain? In the Bible, the name and the person have a very special relationship: they belong to each other. We may know one another's names, but we could have been given a different name. When choosing the names of our children, we come to a short-list of names that we think suitable, and then we finally decide on one. This is not so with God – He and His name are one. His name stands for God Himself. We cannot say when we use His name that we did not mean it. If we happen to be listening to a harmless programme, reading a newspaper article, or listening to a conversation and the name of the Lord is used carelessly or in blasphemy, it has a terrible effect upon us. We go cold and it chills our innermost being because this is the name of our God and Saviour that they are blaspheming and we are unable to bear it.

According to Scripture, when we call on the name of the Lord, we are calling on the Lord Himself. The mention of His name is enough for evil spirits to fear and fly. In *Isaiah 30.27*, we read: 'Behold, the name of the Lord cometh from far', which means that the Lord Himself was coming. In *Acts 2.21*, we read: 'whosoever shall call on the name of the Lord shall be saved.' Clearly, this means calling upon God Himself. In *Mark 9.38*, we read: '...casting out devils in thy name.' The command is associated with the mighty power of the person of Jesus Christ. When we do this, what are we doing? We are using a name, yes, but we are doing more than that: there is the power that is involved in the name of that person. It is not just a magic word like,

'Open, Sesame!', but it is *the Name high over all.* The name involves both the person and the power that the person has.

Perhaps the clearest reference of all is in *Matthew 18.20*: 'For where two or three are gathered together in my name, there am I in the midst of them.' What a comfort! What an encouragement! He is there! If we really believed, when we meet to worship God, that the Lord Himself is there, we would be deeply moved. Imagine a hymn where He is named, He is there! When we pray in His name, He is there!

(3) His Name and His Power

Here is something that we must never forget – the power that is in His name. In our salvation, the name of Jesus Christ is the *only* name that saves. No man comes to the Father any other way. We find this truth clearly stated in *Acts 4.12*: 'Neither is there salvation in any other: for there is none other name under heaven given among men, whereby we must be saved.' When we consider this, we begin to realise the majesty of the Son of God.

This relationship in the Lord Jesus Christ is so very powerful that there is no power on earth or in hell that can break it. When a sinner is justified, he is in Christ, and His name belongs to him. Henceforth, they are inseparable. The apostle Paul speaks of this powerful bond between the Christian and his Lord, in *Romans 8.38-39*: 'For I am persuaded, that neither death, nor life, nor angels, nor principalities, nor powers, nor things present, nor things to come, nor height, nor depth, nor any other creature, shall be able to separate us from the love of God, which is in Christ Jesus our Lord'.

It is a name that enables us to be accepted before the Triune God. It is a name for which we will do anything. Men and women will go out to the furthest corners of the earth for His name's sake. Men will allow themselves to be persecuted and die for His name's sake, because He is so precious to them. There is nothing life can offer that can be compared to the beautiful and eternal relationship between a forgiven sinner and His Saviour. The hymn writer, Charitie Lees de Chenez, understood something of the nature of this eternal bond and the power in that precious name, when she wrote these words:

Before the throne of God above
I have a strong, a perfect plea,
A great High Priest, whose Name is Love,
Who ever lives and pleads for me.

My name is graven in His hands,
My name is written on His heart;
I know that, while in heaven He stands,
No tongue can bid me thence depart.

When Satan tempts me to despair,
And tells me of the guilt within,
Upward I look, and see Him there
Who made an end of all my sin.

God is saying, 'If you would love Me, then you must love Me on My terms.' This is where we find it hard. We should worship Him in spirit and in truth, on His terms. He will give us grace to put Him first and have no other gods. He will give us grace to honour His name. We can treat His name lightly and have a happy-go-lucky evangelical Christianity, but God will not hold us guiltless. Things may go against us, and in our hearts, we can easily become angry with God. We must ask for grace that there may be no anger against His name, and so that we cannot say, 'Why should God do this to me?' We must not use His name thoughtlessly, but with reverence, with love, with adoration and with service. Our lips should honour Him, our hearts adore Him and our lives and our bodies should do anything for His name's sake.

Are we beginning to understand what is expected of us? If we want a God-given revival, then this is the path. 'Love Me', says God, 'on My terms, with a pure and dignified love, with a love that will honour Me, because I will honour them that honour Me.' In this paraphrase of *Hosea 6.1-4*, we are reminded that those who seek to know God and honour Him in their hearts and with their lives, will know much blessing from His hand. The Father seeketh such to worship Him.

Our hearts, if God we seek to know,
Shall know Him and rejoice;
His coming like the morn shall be,
Like morning songs His voice.

As dew upon the tender herb,
Diffusing fragrance round;
As showers that usher in the spring,
And cheer the thirsty ground:

So shall His presence bless our souls,
And shed a joyful light;
That hallowed morn shall chase away
The sorrows of the night.

The Law of Love

Chapter Four

Remember the sabbath day, to keep it holy.
Exodus 20.8

Remember the sabbath day, to keep it holy. Six days shalt thou labour, and do all thy work: but the seventh day is the sabbath of the Lord thy God: in it thou shalt not do any work, thou, nor thy son, nor thy daughter, thy manservant, nor thy maidservant, nor thy cattle, nor thy stranger that is within thy gates: for in six days the Lord made heaven and earth, the sea, and all that in them is, and rested the seventh day: wherefore the Lord blessed the sabbath day, and hallowed it (*Exodus 20.8-11*).

God has appointed a day in which we should remember Him. In a world where the pace of life seems to be increasing daily, it is beneficial to pause and think on our God. It is important for us to remember that there are things ordained by God that we should deeply respect. Yet, we often find that men adopt a legalistic and mechanical attitude to keeping the Lord's Day, which destroys the purpose and the heart of that which God has intended for us. It is also possible to accept the law with gladness, and joyfully fulfil the wish of God with a glad heart, which is an attitude that brings blessing to believers. The blessing and gladness is captured in *Isaiah 58.13*: 'And call the sabbath a delight, the holy of the Lord, honourable'.

In the second chapter of *Genesis*, we are told that when God had finished creating the world, He rested on the seventh day: 'Thus the heavens and the earth were finished, and all the host of them. And on the seventh day God ended his work which he had made; and he rested on the seventh day from all his work which he had made. And God blessed the seventh day, and sanctified it: because that in it he had rested from all his work which God created and made' *(Genesis 2.1-3)*.

The principle of keeping the Sabbath is clearly endorsed in the book of *Leviticus* in a very beautiful way. This principle was expressed by the people in their daily agricultural activity. For six years the land would give of its harvest, but in the seventh year, the land was to remain fallow. This can be seen as a kind of Sabbath for the land. We know by experience in the British Isles how the land was drained of its resources, until crop rotation was implemented and every year a field would remain fallow. As a result, the harvests were richer and therefore the people were happier and their lives more prosperous. The Sabbath shows this same principle. The culmination of the sabbatical years was reached every fiftieth year, and, as we read in *Leviticus 25.9-10*, this was celebrated by the people in a great jubilee: 'Then shalt thou cause the trumpet of the jubile to sound on the tenth day of the seventh month, in the day of atonement shall ye make the trumpet sound throughout all your land. And ye shall hallow the fiftieth year, and proclaim liberty throughout all the land unto all the inhabitants thereof: it shall be a jubile unto you; and ye shall return every man unto his possession, and ye shall return every man unto his family.' It was a time of thanksgiving and faith when the people trusted in the Lord to provide for them, and also a reminder to them that they were not the owners of the land but it was theirs, on trust only. This trust was not to be abused and they had to remember that, as slaves in Egypt, they possessed nothing. Now God had led them to His promised land. It is also salutary to remember that 'the earth is the Lord's, and the fulness thereof.' We are residents, but for a very short time, whatever our status may be.

The jubilee Sabbath was a day of *redemption* when liberty was proclaimed for those in slavery. On the Sabbath, therefore, we remember the cross of our Lord Jesus Christ, which brings freedom to the Christian from the slavery of sin. This jubilee Sabbath was also a day of *restoration.* The people possessed nothing by inherent right. The words of *Deuteronomy 15.15* reminded them that they had been slaves and that the Lord had delivered them from bondage: 'And thou shalt remember that thou wast a bondman in the land of Egypt, and the Lord thy God redeemed thee.' In this year, and in this day of atonement, debts were forgotten and men were restored: '...on the holy day: and that we would leave the seventh year, and the exaction of every debt' *(Nehemiah 10.31).* Many of the hymns that we sing speak of the greatest debt of all that was paid on Calvary, and the freedom that was purchased by Christ for His people:

> *Sing, O sing, of my Redeemer!*
> *With His blood He purchased me,*
> *On the cross He sealed my pardon,*
> *Paid the debt and made me free.*

This Sabbath was a day of *realisation.* There was great joy because so much was fulfilled. It was as if the earth groaned for this Sabbath and rejoiced when this year of fulfilment arrived. In the same way, the New Testament speaks of the great fulfilment of God's plan of redemption at Calvary: 'Because the creature itself also shall be delivered from the bondage of corruption into the glorious liberty of the children of God' *(Romans 8.21).*

In the hope that this brief background study has provided some insight into the Lord's Day, we now come to consider the Sabbath as it appears to Christian people. In previous chapters, we have considered the privilege of the believer in his attitude towards God. Our love should be to God alone and no intruding person or thing should become an image for worship before God. We delight in His name because it is His name and it belongs to Him. It is an all-powerful name, a name at which '*devils fear and fly*'. We honour His person and name, and we worship Him. When we come to His day, God is giving us an opportunity to give an outward expression of our faith and love. We know that our whole life must be a reflection of our glorious faith, but this thing He commands us to do: to remember to keep His day holy. We do not do this in a legalistic way but as an expression of our love. Why do we go to church? Because we love Him. Why do we love Him? Because He first loved us. Love is a stronger motivation than duty. Going to church out of a sense of duty benefits us little, but if we go to church because we love Him, then nothing will stand in our way and stop us from going.

To the Christian, the Sabbath is the Lord's Day, the first day of the week. The believer still honours God's law, but in a very special way and for a very special reason, he remembers the first day of the week. This is the day that the Son of God, the Lord Jesus Christ, rose from the dead. The glorious resurrection is the reason we worship on a Sunday. The honouring of this day has been precious to the believer throughout the long history of the Church. When even a nominal Christian nation loses sight of the observances of this day, it is a sign that it has lost sight of God.

(1) The Command

Do we do things on the Lord's Day that we know, full well, we could do on another day? Then we sin as Christians and our rebuke on the day of Christ will be severe. We can make excuses to one another which are meaningless, but God says that we must keep this day holy and wholly unto Him. How many times do we go to the house of God on a Sunday? Do we say, 'Oh, one service is enough for me?' God says, 'Remember the sabbath day, to keep it holy.' The commandment does not say Sunday morning, it does not say Sunday evening; it says the whole day. We break it if we like, but in the day of Christ we will be answerable. It is the only outward expression that He asks of us, in which we may show our love to Him. There are many ways that this is outworked in our lives.

Why, as Christians, have we changed the day from Saturday to Sunday? It is not just a matter of convenience but of deep significance. The whole of the New Testament supports this change. There is now a covenant of grace and the promises of the Old Testament are fulfilled in the Lord Jesus Christ. Originally, the reason God instituted the Sabbath Day was as a memorial to the creation of the world. It is transferred to the first day of the week in memory of a more glorious work: the re-creation, when Jesus Christ, having fulfilled His great mission of redemption, was raised from the dead. The glory of redemption was greater than that of creation. It is the Lord's Day and has become the Sabbath of the Lord's people.

Great power was used to bring us into being, out of nothing, but greater power was used to bring us out of something worse than nothing – sin. Creation is the work of God's finger; redemption is the work of His arm. In the work of creation, God created man and gave us ourselves, but in redemption, God gave us Himself. In creation, we know of life in Adam; in redemption, we know of life in Christ. In creation, we only learnt of an earthly paradise; in redemption, we learn of a heavenly paradise. It is apparent that the new embraces the old. Furthermore, God is involved in both but in such a way, in His Son, that we stand in awe. It is marvellous in our sight. Therefore, with the authority of the Son of God, we move our day of worship from the seventh day to the first day of the week. It is the Lord's Day, which carries with it the significance of a new life.

What does it mean to keep it holy? 'Holy' originally meant 'separate from other things.' Thus, we separate the Lord's Day from every other day. 'Ah,' but we say, 'we're so busy. We both work and have many children.' Did we create the world? God managed it all in six days! Can we then not order our little lives in six days? It is His wish and His command that we keep the Sabbath. Our normal occupation can take the other days, but our keeping of the Sabbath Day is an open confession that we are the Lord's. Going to church and making the effort to get there even when we do not feel quite up to the mark are both signs that we love Him and delight to obey His command. I am not saying that we go when we are ill because there are times when we cannot make it, but we go whenever possible.

We have all heard of the word 'skimping': it can mean to give or spend too little or only just enough. Do we skimp on His day with sloppy worship and a sloppy attitude to God? Do we skimp on the worship of God? Or, do we with our whole hearts say, 'This is the Lord's Day, here is an opportunity to show my love in an open way.' It should be an expression of our love to God and our devotion to Him that we begin the week with the Lord, seeking His face, and desiring His guidance. To do this is spiritually healthy and robust, and we should do it with a glad and willing heart. The keeping of this day has a profound effect upon society, as it constantly reminds the unbeliever of God Himself and of His people.

(2) The Consideration

The Christian has the privilege of remembering the Lord's Day. In its observance, there is both a negative and a positive aspect to be considered. The week is planned out for us by God, and in His wisdom He guides us in the way that is both right and best. This is what we are told in the fourth commandment: 'Six days shalt thou labour, and do all thy work: but the seventh day is the sabbath of the Lord thy God: in it thou shalt not do any work, thou, nor thy son, nor thy daughter, thy manservant, nor thy maidservant, nor thy cattle, nor thy stranger that is within thy gates: for in six days the Lord made heaven and earth, the sea, and all that in them is, and rested the seventh day: wherefore the Lord blessed the sabbath day, and hallowed it' (Exodus 20.9-11).

It is true that we live in a society that totally disregards any Christian principles, thus making it very difficult for a Christian to adhere to this law as much as perhaps he would like to. How then do we face the situation? We begin with an attitude of determination that the day will not be spent in those things that can be done on other days. However, deeds of necessity and mercy are allowed, but nothing else. A person knows in his heart if his action is harmless and honest before God, yet in this determination, he must not be legalistic. In *Mark 2*, we read the account of the disciples, who were observed by the Pharisees while plucking corn as they went through the fields on the Sabbath. The Pharisees always interpreted everything so literally that they lost the spirit and the real meaning of the matter. In this account, our Lord points out to them how wrong they are to judge the disciples: 'And the Pharisees said unto him, Behold, why do they on the sabbath day that which is not lawful? And he said unto them, Have ye never read what David did, when he had need, and was an hungred, he, and they that were with him? How he went into the house of God in the days of Abiathar the high priest, and did eat the shewbread, which is not lawful to eat but for the priests, and gave also to them which were with him? And he said unto them, The sabbath was made for man, and not man for the sabbath: therefore the Son of man is Lord also of the sabbath' *(Mark 2.24-28)*.

It is, however, the positive aspect of the law that makes keeping the Lord's Day a great joy. We are to make it a separate day, and separated as unto the Lord. With our lips, we honour God; with our hearts, we adore Him; with our bodies, we obey Him. It is good to encourage one another in this expression of our faith and love, as we are exhorted to do in *Hebrews 10.24-25*: 'And let us consider one another to provoke unto love and to good works: not forsaking the assembling of ourselves together, as the manner of some is; but exhorting one another: and so much the more, as ye see the day approaching.' All this we do in the light of that great day, and in the light of eternity.

Note the reference to assembling together. It is true that we have individual responsibilities to keep our devotional times because our faith in Christ is a personal one. Nevertheless, we are part of the body of Christ, so we must consider the corporate body. On this one day of the week, most particularly, we do this good thing and we consider seriously and honestly the law of God for His day.

He does not ask much of us. He says, 'If you love Me, keep My day.' We might ask, 'What hast Thou done to deserve my love, O God?' 'I gave my Son, because I so loved the world, that whosoever believeth in Him should not perish but have everlasting life.' Was there anything that deserved a day more than that? Is there anything that should melt our hearts more than that? Is there any motive that should drive us to come to worship God together, more than that? If persecution comes against us, we will still come together to worship. If swords come against us, we will go through the swords to reach the house of God, even if we come bleeding to church. Why? Because of Calvary. Let us fulfil the one request He asks of us and keep this day wholly unto Him.

(3) The Communion

In our minds, we should consider the eternal Sabbath and the rest that awaits the people of God. The keeping of the Lord's Day on earth is a reflection of the joy to come. In a madly busy world, we quieten ourselves and make our way with our brothers and sisters to the house of the Lord. In a determined way, we set our faces towards God. By doing so, we honour Him. Everything militates against it, but we do this good thing because it is His will.

There are benefits in the observance of His day. It is well pleasing in the sight of God and it is deeply satisfying to our hearts and souls. When we come to worship Him willingly, with deep reverence, in spirit and in truth, every part of the service is rich to our souls. From the deep recesses of our being, there arises the incense of adoration as we read the Word, pray to Him and sing the psalms and hymns. Not only do we have fellowship with one another but also, in a way, we join with Christians of all lands and with those who are already in the Sabbath of glory. It should be our greatest delight to be in the house of the Lord on His day, and our greatest fear should be our absence. We must not forsake assembling together for we, like Thomas, who was absent from that first meeting after the resurrection when Christ appeared to His disciples, might miss out on a blessing which the Lord has for us. It is an exciting occupation and perhaps the one thing that is nearest to heaven on earth. We are able to have communion with God when we are on our own, but this we do together as the people of the Lord, and there is something special about it.

We live in ungodly days. To attend the house of God on the Lord's Day is a great witness to an ungodly people and also a reminder to them of God and the judgement to come. Let us, therefore, make our Sabbath worship a public thing before the world and encourage one another. It is not hard if we look at Calvary. It is not hard if we think of eternity. It is satisfying to gather together as a people of the Lord and to worship Him. Our friends are there, our kindred are there. If anyone will help in time of trouble, we will find them there in the family of God. Those who will hold us up in a time of trial, we will find there. It is also a great witness wherever a church is open on the Lord's Day, for whenever the people of God gather together, the unbeliever knows. They see us going there. We may not know that we are being observed, but we are. They see our doors opening at a certain time each Sunday and they know where we are going. We cannot deceive ourselves and think that if we live in a big city, people will not know our business. They know! The people in the streets, the roads, the avenues where we live, all know how regularly we go to church; they will watch how it affects us on the remaining six days of the week.

'Remember the Sabbath day, to keep it holy,' is the command. Do this, and we will experience His keeping power in wonderful ways in our lives. If we honour Him, He will honour us. He does not ask much, but if we do it, we will begin to see something happening in our lives. Our attitudes will change and we will be filled with the love of God. As we submit ourselves to the Word of God, we will find it is not hard or heavy, but easy and pleasant and good.

O worship the Lord in the beauty of holiness;
Bow down before Him, His glory proclaim;
With gold of obedience and incense of lowliness,
Kneel and adore Him, the Lord is His Name.

Low at His feet lay thy burden of carefulness;
High on His heart He will bear it for thee,
Comfort thy sorrows, and answer thy prayerfulness,
Guiding thy steps as may best for thee be.

Fear not to enter His courts in the slenderness
Of the poor wealth thou wouldst reckon as thine;
Truth in its beauty and love in its tenderness,
These are the offerings to lay on His shrine.

These, though we bring them in trembling and fearfulness,
He will accept for the Name that is dear;
Mornings of joy give for evenings of tearfulness,
Trust for our trembling, and hope for our fear.

O worship the Lord in the beauty of holiness;
Bow down before Him, His glory proclaim;
With gold of obedience and incense of lowliness,
Kneel and adore Him, the Lord is His Name.

John Samuel Bewley Monsell.

The Law of Love

Chapter Five

**Honour thy father
and thy mother.**
Exodus 20.12

**Honour thy father and thy mother: that thy days may be long upon
the land which the Lord thy God giveth thee** *(Exodus 20.12).*

The Ten Commandments are divided into two parts. We have
already looked at the commandments that refer to God Himself, the
worship of God, and the honouring of His name and His day. Now we
will consider those commandments that refer to our relationship with
one another, and our attitudes to one another, as men and women of
grace. Such commandments carry a challenge as it is expressed in
1 John 4.20-21: 'If a man say, I love God, and hateth his brother, he is
a liar: for he that loveth not his brother whom he hath seen, how can
he love God whom he hath not seen? And this commandment have we
from him, that he who loveth God love his brother also.' In other
words, we shall consider what the substance of loving our neighbour
really means. It will seem as if we are listing some negative principles,
but in fact, we are making a positive statement. In this section we shall
be thinking particularly of our Lord and Saviour Jesus Christ: His life,

His example and all that He is. We must remember that the Lord Jesus Christ fulfilled the law of God and is the supreme example to His followers. We must also remember, as born again believers, that we are now given the grace to fulfil these laws that we once found so impossible. The reason for this is that the Lord Jesus Christ lives in us, and our lives must be an outshining of His blessed person and ways. We find at last, by God's grace, that we have the ability to love someone other than ourselves.

The Top and the Bottom of the Ladder

A lovely illustration, given by one of the Puritans, is helpful here. He talks of a ladder, the base of which is firmly fixed in grace and the top enters into glory. It has ten rungs, ten steps to heaven. We try to climb that ladder and cannot, so the Lord Jesus Christ does it for us: He climbs the ladder and He fulfils the law of God on our behalf. He also pays the penalty for our failure, and then He comes down that ladder by the Holy Spirit and gives us grace to believe. He holds our hand and takes us up the ladder, right to the very top, and says, 'Behold your God.' Then He brings us back down the ladder and says, 'Live on earth until I take you up the ladder for the last time and take you home.' It is a very lovely picture.

Honour amidst Dishonour

We are living in a very unruly age where there is no respect at all for authority: to governments of countries, to the keeping of law and order and the demands made by the authorities of countries. In school there is no respect paid to head teachers and school teachers. Even within the church, little respect is paid to the fathers of the faith. The Ten Commandments, by contrast, are a foretaste of heaven, an eternal Sabbath, where we shall worship God alone, in spirit and in truth, and honour His name. If we really love God and seek to keep the first four commandments, we will bow to His authority and try to keep the other six while we are here on earth. We will be enabled to do so by His grace, and thereby, experience a foretaste of heaven.

(1) The Home

The greatest test of this love towards one another is in the home. Whatever the circumstances of the home may be, it is there that we are seen for what we really are. It is easy for us to be on our best behaviour in public but what are we like at home? We are known there by our families and we know them. A husband and wife know each other very well. Parents and children are well acquainted with each other and sometimes children have a very astute way of summing up their parents. However young our children are, they get to know us well. They know the different facets to our personalities, and we know our children. Our relatives are quick to point out our failings, especially our lack of love! This can be very provocative and usually powerfully true. Nevertheless, a few home truths may drive us the more to seek the grace of God in our lives.

Today, Satan is shattering homes with division and discontentment. Somehow, the Christian must do what is right in the midst of the ruin of present-day society. We have God on our side and He is able to perform great things. What a joy it would be to see these well-known words applied to our family lives: 'Christ is the Head of this house, the silent Guest at every meal, the unseen Listener to every conversation.' Some of us will find this fifth commandment very easy because we have lovely parents; others will find it hard because we do not have easy parents. But, whatever our circumstances, He asks us to honour them.

We can take the legalistic attitude of the Pharisees and miss the heart of the message. In *Mark 7.9-13*, we read how Christ spoke to the Pharisees about their wrong approach in applying this commandment: 'And he said unto them, Full well ye reject the commandment of God, that ye may keep your own tradition. For Moses said, Honour thy father and thy mother; and, Whoso curseth father or mother, let him die the death: but ye say, If a man shall say to his father or mother, It is Corban, that is to say, a gift, by whatsoever thou mightest be profited by me; he shall be free. And ye suffer him no more to do ought for his father or his mother; making the word of God of none effect through your tradition, which ye have delivered: and many such like things do ye.' This is a pharisaical way of dealing with the commandment, where we might say, 'Here are my parents, here is a gift and I have given my nominal due to my father and mother.' If we take this attitude, then we dismiss what is required of the law, which is to honour them. We should note that the minimum requirement is to honour. We are, of course, allowed to give much more but the commandment is allowing for a sinful world where we may have very difficult parents. We see this requirement again in the epistle to the *Ephesians 6.2-3*: 'Honour thy father and mother; (which is the first commandment with promise;) that it may be well with thee, and thou mayest live long on the earth.' We are to show them respect. If we belong to a spiritually mixed family this can be very difficult; yet in as far as we are able, in the sight of God, we must honour our parents.

In the context of the home, there is another aspect to this relationship, of which we read in the next verse of *Ephesians 6*: 'And, ye fathers, provoke not your children to wrath: but bring them up in the nurture and admonition of the Lord' *(Ephesians 6.4)*. All this is a help towards the peace of a home. Peace is a rare jewel today and well worth cherishing. Although we are mainly concerned with honouring fathers and mothers in this chapter, at the same time, in a Christian home, it is worthwhile remembering that, as parents, we must not be provocative and make it difficult for our children to honour us.

How can a Christian father make it difficult for his children to honour him? By making the Christian faith a real burden to them. We should keep family worship but we should be considerate towards the children. Children are very strange and wonderful beings; they learn more by example than by rule. Children desire to be like their parents and, before long, when they see us bow our heads in prayer, they will want to do the same. Eventually, we will find that the children want to sit around with us and take their place at family worship; they want to read their verse and they feel it an honour to take part. We must also respect their independence. There are dangerous things we must tell them not to do, but there is also an area where they have to find out things for themselves. As they grow older, we can tell them: 'I don't believe that it is right, but you must decide for yourself.' We must respect them too, as personalities, so let us not make the burden of our faith so heavy upon them that they will use the excuse that many people use today: 'I was made to go to church.' At the same time, it is ridiculous to say to a child, 'You can come to chapel if you like.' That is foolish. If we are a Christian family, we will want to bring them to church and, at the same time, show them that we love to come. We must make our faith a lovely and a joyous thing because we desire to win their honour.

Honouring our parents is not a hard commandment, when we have grace in our hearts. We not only honour them, but we can love them and do many things for them. However, many people are not so blessed; they have parents who are antagonistic towards them and who seem to hate their own children. What do we do then? Do not despise them. As Christians, let us ask God for grace to honour them and respect them as people. Let us see the wisdom of God. Some parents are very demanding and others are difficult, but we must still honour and respect them. This is the minimum requirement but it is wonderful if we can go further and give even more.

(2) The Heart

A question may arise in our hearts: 'How can I ever achieve this in my life and my home?' The answer is that you cannot, apart from the grace of God. But even then, the battle is lost and won in the heart of the Christian. We have to face these things spiritually, as we are exhorted to do in *Philippians 2.12*: '...work out your own salvation with fear and trembling.' We must think and work out how we ought to behave in a given situation as a Christian. There are some parents who make demands on their children and who come between husband and wife; such situations have to be worked out without being hurtful to our parents. Our first duty should be to our partner, and yet we must honour our father and mother. There are many and varied situations that we must work out spiritually in our hearts, knowing, before God, that we are honest in this. We know the Scriptures and we know the will of God. The amazing thing is that, when we have this co-operation in our hearts and minds, God steps in: 'For it is God which worketh in you both to will and to do of his good pleasure' *(Philippians 2.13).*

As Christian people, we must always endeavour to do that which is right. It may be respect for our parents that will be the means of their eventually honouring God the Father, by coming to Jesus Christ as Saviour. The battle for the home is in the heart, because if these principles are not present, then our heart is not genuine. Our attitude must not be: 'Ok, I will keep this commandment and nobody will be able to point a finger at me. I've done my duty by my parents.' We might say of the Pharisees that they did their duty and yet in their heart there was no honour. Let us ask God for grace upon grace that we might keep this commandment truly and genuinely from the heart.

(3) The Hope

This is the first commandment with promise: 'that thy days may be *long* upon the land which the Lord thy God giveth thee.' The quotation in *Ephesians* differs slightly from the one in *Exodus*: 'that it may be *well* with thee, and thou mayest live *long* on the earth.' We are all aware of the teaching that prevailed in the times of the Old Testament dispensation. It was the common belief that a good man would live long and flourish and that the wicked would suffer. Job's friends were quick to point out that, in the midst of all his sufferings, somehow he had failed badly. The book of *Job* dispels this wrong notion. Trials are not necessarily consequences of sins, and prosperity is not necessarily a consequence of godliness. Indeed, we are aware that good children who believe in God, and who honour and obey their parents, can die young. What can we say? We cannot give a glib answer as to why a young life is sometimes, as is often said, 'cut short'. Perhaps it is right and proper to point out that our only certainty is, not of a long life, but an eternal one! 'It will be *well* with thee.' What a glad and welcome word!

In such circumstances, we might say with Job: 'Oh that my words were now written! oh that they were printed in a book! That they were graven with an iron pen and lead in the rock for ever! For I know that my redeemer liveth, and that he shall stand at the latter day upon the earth: and though after my skin worms destroy this body, yet in my flesh shall I see God: whom I shall see for myself, and mine eyes shall behold, and not another; though my reins be consumed within me' *(Job 19.23-27)*.

The Bottom of the Ladder

We must also remember the day of Christ: 'For we must all appear before the judgment seat of Christ; that every one may receive the things done in his body, according to that he hath done, whether it be good or bad' *(2 Corinthians 5.10)*. It may be well with us now and in that day. In as far as we can, we should live a life where we have no regrets in our attitude to one another, so that we may enter into glory with a mind at peace, in the grace of Christ, and a lovely obedience to the law of love. Imagine if God should pay a visit to our homes to see if we are honouring our parents: would it be well with us? Let us remind ourselves that He loved us so that we might be able to love Him and love one another. One day we shall be with Him in glory, and will have to give Him an account of our family life.

How shall we respond to this godly obligation? Let me mention again the ladder described by the Puritan. We have gone up the ladder and we see that, in Christ, all is complete. Then we come down the ladder again and we are here on earth. We might then ask, 'What shall we do, Lord, that it might be well with us?' 'I want you to have a foretaste of heaven; I want your church and your family to be a little heaven; I want you to love Me only; I want you to worship Me in spirit and in truth; I want you to honour My name; I want you to keep My day and meet together to worship Me; I want you to honour your father and mother and then it will be well with you,' is our Lord's reply.

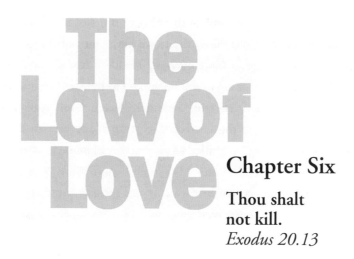

The Law of Love

Chapter Six

Thou shalt not kill.
Exodus 20.13

In the Ten Commandments, we begin with our love towards God, as believers. This love overflows into every part of our lives so that not only do we love our neighbour, but we are given enabling grace to love our enemies as well. In *1 John 4.20*, we read that it is impossible for the Christian to love God and not love his fellow man: 'If a man say, I love God, and hateth his brother, he is a liar: for he that loveth not his brother whom he hath seen, how can he love God whom he hath not seen?' It may seem strange that this commandment is here at all, but we have only to look at the history of the world, and sadly at the history of nominal Christendom, to understand the necessity of this commandment. We shall consider more deeply the meaning of killing as explained to us in the Scriptures.

(1) The Sin of Anger

Anger is a very dangerous thing. Who can tell to what it may lead and where it will end? The shedding of a man's blood and the taking of a life is regarded seriously by God. Something of the seriousness of the crime is touched on in *Genesis 9.6*, where we are reminded that every man is made in the image of God: 'Whoso sheddeth man's blood, by man shall his blood be shed: for in the image of God made he man.' In the account of Cain and Abel in *Genesis 4*, when Cain took his brother's life, the words of the Lord in Scripture are severe: 'And he said, What hast thou done? the voice of thy brother's blood crieth unto me from the ground' *(Genesis 4.10)*.

The New Testament certainly confirms the serious nature of the crime. The Lord Jesus Christ, in the Sermon on the Mount, said: 'Ye have heard that it was said by them of old time, Thou shalt not kill; and whosoever shall kill shall be in danger of the judgment: but I say unto you, That whosoever is angry with his brother without a cause shall be in danger of the judgment: and whosoever shall say to his brother, Raca, shall be in danger of the council: but whosoever shall say, Thou fool, shall be in danger of hell fire' *(Matthew 5.21-22)*. We now come to the application of this commandment to the believer. A man's life is a very sacred and holy thing, and we should never regard it lightly. We may ask, 'But how can we apply this to the Christian?' There are other ways of killing, apart from taking a person's life.

We can kill another person by killing his reputation and his good name with gossip. It can be with words so cruel and unkind that it is as if we have murdered him. What we said may have been true, but no thanks to us for passing it on. It may not have been true, but we have murdered, we have killed, and caused a person to suffer a living death.

We can kill a person by misrepresenting him. We can say something about him that will so damage his character that he is completely discredited for years, maybe for the rest of his life.

We can kill a person's spirit. We can daunt and discourage him, or we can neglect to encourage him. We can say a word that will go like a shaft into his heart and, although he may say nothing about it to us, we have killed him. We have killed his spirit.

As Christian people, with the grace of God in our hearts, we must be so careful to let grace prevail. James reminds us of the great damage a word can do: 'Even so the tongue is a little member, and boasteth great things. Behold, how great a matter a little fire kindleth! And the tongue is a fire, a world of iniquity: so is the tongue among our members, that it defileth the whole body, and setteth on fire the course of nature; and it is set on fire of hell ... the tongue can no man tame; it is an unruly evil, full of deadly poison' *(James 3. 5-8)*.

When the heart is lacking in grace, the tongue is an unruly member. It can be sharper than a sword and, in modern terms, it can be more savage than a bullet. It can be terribly penetrating. It is just a small member, but what a fire it can kindle! What damage a word can do! It can cause a stir in society about a person or, quietly, can place doubt in a person's heart. Yes, this verse applies to the Christian. We must be careful not to be 'trigger happy'. We find it so easy to say, 'I'll put them right! Let me have a word!' Let us be watchful; we are dealing with people's immortal souls. The simple answer is to examine our own hearts and see that our motives are honourable, pure and right in everything we do.

(2) The Source of Anger

We are new men in Christ; the old man is crucified. Nevertheless, we have to contend with the flesh. The dreadful potential of the flesh is graphically described in *James 4.1-2*: 'From whence come wars and fightings among you? come they not hence, even of your lusts that war in your members? Ye lust, and have not: ye kill, and desire to have, and cannot obtain: ye fight and war, yet ye have not, because ye ask not.'

Why do these things happen? James is saying that because we do not ask for grace, we do not receive. The epistle to the *Colossians* tells us to be what we are in Christ: 'And have put on the new man, which is renewed in knowledge after the image of him that created him' *(Colossians 3.10)*. The instruction in the epistle to the *Ephesians* is very clear regarding our behaviour in this matter: 'And that ye put on the new man, which after God is created in righteousness and true holiness. Wherefore putting away lying, speak every man truth with his neighbour: for we are members one of another. Be ye angry, and sin not: let not the sun go down upon your wrath' *(Ephesians 4.24-26).* Even righteous anger is not allowed to fester and become an ugly thing.

Let us remember what we are. When we were unconverted, our innermost being ruled in complete harmony with the flesh, the flesh being the totality of what we are as human beings. Nevertheless, when we are converted, the old man is transformed and becomes the new man, without loss of identity. The new man loves God, but still has to contend with the flesh and its desires. However, a radical change has taken place and the new man is able to draw on the vast resources of God at his disposal. It is a shame to live as spiritual paupers when we are princes by right. *Romans 6.6* tells us that we are not what we once were. We are no longer slaves to sin: 'Knowing this, that our old man is crucified with him, that the body of sin might be destroyed, that henceforth we should not serve sin.' The flesh wars against the spirit and lusts spring from there. We have, however, no excuse, as the strength of God is ours and the new man is in the image of God. When men boast of their bad tempers and hasty tongues and, at the same time, claim to be Christians, they are giving in to the flesh and failing to follow the ways of the Lord.

(3) The Solution of Anger

What shall we do with this great problem that so easily besets us and rushes so rapidly into our hearts? Before we know where we are, the hasty, cruel word and wicked action has taken place and we have dishonoured the name of our Lord. Surely, we should dread this. Let us remember that Satan knows the weakness of our flesh and, like a roaring lion, lying in wait to attack, he will seize his opportunity to provoke the flesh.

We are conscious that we are new creatures in Christ and that our behaviour must be consistent with our position. We must learn to withstand the onslaughts of the flesh and recognise the wiles of the devil, refusing to allow anything to deprive us of our peace. How soon we forget the source of our strength and do not make use of the means that are at our disposal! In *James 4.2*, we are reminded again of our neglect in this area: '…ye have not, because ye ask not.'

Let us remember that records are kept in heaven. Imagine for a moment that we are there. The records are opened and we read that, at one time, we had a difficulty and we began to grow cold towards God. We began to go back into our old sins and yet we knew that we were Christians. 'When did this situation happen?' we are asked. The records are consulted again, 'But you did not bring it to the throne of grace in order to obtain mercy and grace to help in time of need. There is no record of your asking, and that is why you did not receive.' If only we were more accustomed to practising the presence of God and keeping in close fellowship with our Saviour, many of the problems that we encounter in our lives would not arise. When we consider the perfection of His character, and that this Saviour abides with us and keeps close to our hearts, then we have every opportunity to become more than conquerors in every situation. Let us turn our eyes upon the Lord Jesus Christ, 'Who, when he was reviled, reviled not again; when he suffered, he threatened not; but committed himself to him that judgeth righteously' *(1 Peter 2.23)*.

In this new life, as Christian people, we learn a reverence for life and a respect for people. We become aware of our own needs and understand the needs of others. We begin to understand that irritation and anger are no solution. A strong understanding and a sympathetic heart, born of a humble spirit, is the Christian way.

In *Acts 7*, Stephen, when he had fearlessly condemned the sin of the people and graciously preached the Gospel, forgave those who were killing him, by asking the Lord not to lay this sin against them. Here we see grace in action. In the Sermon on the Mount, the Lord Jesus Christ desires that we go all the way with Him and exhorts us to love our enemies: 'But I say unto you, Love your enemies, bless them that curse you, do good to them that hate you, and pray for them which despitefully use you, and persecute you; that ye may be the children of your Father which is in heaven' *(Matthew 5.44-45).*

How can this happen? The secret is to live near the Saviour and to delight in Him, ever desiring to do that which is well-pleasing in His sight. Let us commit it unto Him who judgeth righteously and He will give us these positive things: God's grace to love and forgive, and a respect and a reverence for life.

Take my life, and let it be
Consecrated, Lord, to Thee:
Take my moments and my days,
Let them flow in ceaseless praise.

Take my hands, and let them move
At the impulse of Thy love:
Take my feet, and let them be
Swift and beautiful for Thee.

Take my voice, and let me sing,
Always, only, for my King:
Take my lips, and let them be
Filled with messages from Thee.

Take my silver and my gold;
Not a mite would I withhold:
Take my intellect, and use
Every power as Thou shalt choose.

Take my will, and make it Thine;
It shall be no longer mine:
Take my heart, it is Thine own;
It shall be Thy royal throne.

Take my love; my Lord, I pour
At Thy feet its treasure-store:
Take myself, and I will be,
Ever, only, all for Thee!

Frances Ridley Havergal

The Law of Love

Chapter Seven

Thou shalt not commit adultery.
Exodus 20.14

How very far the ways and laws of a land can go from the ways and laws of our God! When this happens, distress comes to the lives of many, and disorder and chaos to the life of the community and the nation in general. Great concern has been expressed about the decline of family life and the sorrow of children who have never known the love of a happy home; yet we live in a time when that which is lawlessness in God's sight is encouraged, and that which is lawful and good is discouraged. In *Isaiah 5.20*, the words of Scripture warn against such attitudes: 'Woe unto them that call evil good, and good evil; that put darkness for light, and light for darkness; that put bitter for sweet, and sweet for bitter!'. It is utter folly to disregard God, for it brings nothing but unhappiness and sorrow in this life, and, for the Christian, shame in the day of Christ. We must honour God's law and observe the sanctity of the moral code that God has laid before us in His Word.

Adultery has always been an unhappy subject, and it is particularly so, in our day. The present statistics are horrifying, and uncertainty and instability in the home has become common. Indeed, it is as if marriage were an experiment rather than a life together. The days are evil: everything militates against the Christian view of marriage, and it is particularly difficult for young people who are brought up in this lax environment.

It seems that some Christians, despite having had an experience of the grace of God, want to love God and their neighbour on their own terms. Many years ago, John Bunyan said, 'I walk by the rule of my Master. You walk by the rude working of your fancies.' We should truly desire to walk with God in the way that He wants us to walk – we find this way set out for us, in the Scriptures. We are not allowed to take away, nor are we allowed to add to the words of Scripture. It is to the Scriptures alone as the revealed Word of God that we must look. We will find that the Bible tells us, 'Thou shalt not commit adultery.' With the Scriptures in mind, we would do well to pay attention to the opening words of this well-known hymn by John Henry Sammis:

> *When we walk with the Lord*
> *In the light of His Word,*
> *What a glory He sheds on our way!*

(1) The Vow

Before we can begin to think about the meaning of adultery, we must have a right view of marriage and a high regard for the marriage vows. What is a vow but a solemn promise that we make before God? In the Scriptures, we are told that marriage is so sacred that it is like the marriage of the Son to His redeemed people. This elevated comparison is defined in the epistle to the *Ephesians 5.24-27*: 'Therefore as the church is subject unto Christ, so let the wives be to their own husbands in every thing. Husbands, love your wives, even as Christ also loved the church, and gave himself for it; that he might sanctify and cleanse it with the washing of water by the word, that he might present it to himself a glorious church, not having spot, or wrinkle, or any such thing; but that it should be holy and without blemish.'

This is the supreme example. How much did Jesus Christ love His church? He gave Himself for it. What does this mean? Motivated by the love of God, it cost Him to be joined to the Church. This is spelled out for us in the same epistle: 'But now in Christ Jesus ye who sometimes were far off are made nigh by the blood of Christ' *(Ephesians 2.13)*. This is how much He loves. He is willing to make His bride, the Church, fit for His Father's home. He is willing to make her clean and so He takes upon Himself her sin, her iniquity, her burdens, everything, and pays the penalty. Why does He do this? So that His bride may be dressed in white. So that His bride may be without spot or blemish, redeemed by His blood. This is our pattern: He, the glorious Son of God, is the Bridegroom; we, the Church, are His bride. Where did she get her wedding dress? Where was she made clean? She was washed in the blood of the Saviour. Where was she pardoned? In the wounds of Christ. Where was she found? In an alien land. What did He give her? He dressed her with His own imputed righteousness. She is dressed in glorious, white apparel, ready to be presented in that day, before God the Father. Adultery, then, is a very serious thing.

When we consider these Scriptures, we are bound to be impressed by the status of marriage. If it is important in God's eyes, then it should be important in our eyes. Marriage is ordained of God and is an institution for mankind, but most particularly for the Christian, to honour. What is more, we make our promises before God.

(2) The Violation

So far, we have considered the sanctity of marriage and its preciousness in the sight of God. The breakdown of trust when one's partner commits adultery is a very sad thing in itself, and very far reaching in its effect. The repercussions of a broken home grieve the children and the extended families of the couple in question, as well as the couple themselves. It is altogether a sorrowful thing. When marriage is allowed to break down from that which God has ordained, it causes distress and grief. Such sorrow has resulted in the employment of an ever-increasing number of social workers and marriage counsellors. Furthermore, successive governments have been responsible for passing laws contrary to that which God has ordained for all mankind. This has added to the misery of our land.

The insight provided by the Lord Jesus Christ into the source of this problem is very searching. He examines the heart of the individual, where adultery begins. We see this in the words of Christ, in *Matthew 5.27-28*: 'Ye have heard that it was said by them of old time, Thou shalt not commit adultery: but I say unto you, That whosoever looketh on a woman to lust after her hath committed adultery with her already in his heart.'

In the Old Testament, we are given the example of King David who caused such grief in this matter. He noticed the beauty of Bath-sheba, wife to Uriah, and desired her in his heart. We could say that he did not commit adultery with her then. But he did in his heart, and he found the time to actually commit adultery with her later. She was another man's wife and he had no right to her. Knowing that his sin had been exposed, he devised a scheme to get rid of Uriah by putting him on the front line of battle, making sure of his death. David fulfilled the desire of his heart but brought the displeasure of God upon his action. The Psalm that is associated with his repentance is *Psalm 51*: 'Wash me throughly from mine iniquity, and cleanse me from my sin. For I acknowledge my transgressions: and my sin is ever before me. Against thee, thee only, have I sinned, and done this evil in thy sight' *(Psalm 51.2-4)*.

What the Lord Jesus Christ is saying is that we must guard our hearts. How does this affect our view of marriage? Do not enter into it thoughtlessly or lightly, but reverently, discreetly and in the fear of God. The violation of this sacred vow breaks the covenant. If we follow the guidance of the Lord Jesus Christ and refuse to allow iniquity in our hearts, then we are far less likely to bring this grief upon ourselves.

Another Violation

Today, we live in an unfaithful age and society. Previously, society was influenced by the benefits of Christianity. Now, it is a very different matter. Even well known denominations condone sins that are great violations in the sight of God, even to the extent of condoning adultery. It is as if the Church is saying to the world, 'We deny the deity of Christ. We deny the virgin birth.' Many of the leaders of these churches have been saying these things for a long time, but they have not let the people know what they really believed. They have kept an 'orthodox' front. Books have been written that have created a sensation amongst the people, yet all these books have done is to express publicly what the leaders of many churches have believed, and what has been taught in many theological colleges, for over half a century! It would have been far better if these men had been honest and said, 'We were never called. There was never any grace in our hearts.'

Can we allow such a violation? Can we co-exist with such adultery? Can we turn our backs upon our Bridegroom, upon the Rose of Sharon, the Lily of the Valley, the Fairest of Ten Thousand to our souls? Can we turn our backs on Him and flirt with the philosophies of the world?

(3) The Victory

Returning to our main theme of marital adultery, we must recognise that there will never be a time when marriages will not break down. There is, however, a great difference in this being the exception rather than the rule. Since this is a spiritual union in the sight of God, then we should do all that we can to maintain the sanctity of marriage.

It begins with our attitude to courtship. If there is a lack of respect for one another, and if we treat intimate relationships lightly, then we will not suddenly change when we get married. In the words of the marriage vows, we read that marriage is not to be entered into thoughtlessly, but reverently, and in the fear of God. It is a good and robust thing to make friendships in groups of young men and women. However, when a young man singles out a young lady for his special attention, there must also be a spiritual attitude in both of them towards the relationship. Also there must be a spiritual compatibility that allows them to share in the same experience of the grace of God. To consider a relationship that leads to matrimony with an unconverted person is wrong. There is no guarantee that the unbelieving partner will come the way of the believer. Indeed, it is easier to drag the Christian down, into compromise, than it is to pull the unbeliever out of the darkness of unbelief. Eventually, however tolerant the unbelieving partner may be, it will lead to many problems.

There must also be mutual attraction. God has given us bodies and made us male and female. Unless we are attracted to each other, we are making a great mistake. We are either attracted or we are not, and that is the sum total of the matter. To overlook this makes any marriage difficult.

Then there is friendship. Unless we get on with each other and have plenty to say to one another, then the relationship will be very boring indeed and can only spell disaster. A life together is full of sharing and caring for one another and being interested in the details of the life that we have together. We must enjoy each other's company; our interests need not be identical but we can share them.

How can we have this victory? It is going to cost because love is always costly. We must always remember that the relationship between the Church and Christ is our aim and pattern; marriage is our situation. Between the Church and Christ, there should be that lovely unity of faith, obedience and love. The principles of marriage are set out for us in the epistle to the *Ephesians*: 'So ought men to love their wives as their own bodies' *(Ephesians 5.28)*.

How many times have we heard it stressed that the wife should obey her husband but neglecting the fact that the husband has to love his wife. The responsibility is on both husband and wife. How much must a husband love his wife? He must give himself. In the marriage service he has said, 'I give myself unto thee and to thee alone ...' He must give himself and the love of his heart. If he wants to know how, then he must, '*Turn (his) eyes upon Jesus, and look full in His wonderful face.*' He must consider the redemptive love of Christ. Look at the connection between husband and wife, and between Christ and the Church, in *Ephesians 5.31-32*: 'For this cause shall a man leave his father and mother, and shall be joined unto his wife, and they two shall be one flesh. This is a great mystery: but I speak concerning Christ and the church.' His love to his wife must be patterned on that sacrificial love. It is a love that does not hold back. It is a complete love.

It does not stop there, as we see in *Ephesians 5.22*: 'Wives, submit yourselves unto your own husbands, as unto the Lord.' In the same way as the husband must take Christ as his pattern, so the wife must submit 'as unto the Lord'. Remember, the husband loves his wife as Christ loves His Church. It is not difficult for the Church to obey a Saviour who bled on Calvary for her. It is not difficult or unreasonable for the wife to obey a husband who loves her with a Christ-like love. Submit as unto the Lord. Many object to this teaching, but I offer it to you as the secret of keeping the marriage.

However difficult or lovely a husband or wife may be, we must not commit adultery, either physically or in our hearts. How shall we do this? We are able to do this because we have been made new, as we find it expressed in *2 Corinthians 5.17*: 'Therefore if any man be in Christ, he is a new creature: old things are passed away; behold, all things are become new.' God gives us the grace to love one another. I am not saying it lightly, but we do need grace, even in the best of homes; we need grace, and grace upon grace. May God give us, as His children, that grace.

The Law of Love

Chapter Eight

Thou shalt not steal.
Exodus 20.15

Loving our neighbour is a very positive thing, as we learn from the pattern of behaviour set out for us by God. There is another thing about which we must be careful, and that is not to steal. In our day, when honesty has virtually disappeared, there is a great need for honest men and women. Dishonesty and stealing ruin character, spoil relationships and grieve the Spirit of God.

Honesty is a deep and a pure thing; it is a right attitude of heart. Becoming a thief on any level ruins this very beautiful thing. In society, stealing is obnoxious, and amongst Christians, it should not even be considered. A Christian, because of the love in his heart, will honour his parents and will not even contemplate a murderous thought. He will not have an adulterous mind or commit an adulterous action and will endeavour, by God's grace, to be an honest man. To live such a life is worthwhile and is God-honouring, as well as being a challenge to the world we live in.

The commandments may seem to be negative, but their teaching is positive. It is positive to be a person of honesty and integrity. The commandments contain plenty to occupy our minds and our hearts, and they create a desire to fill our lives with doing what is right. In his epistle to the *Ephesians*, the apostle Paul encourages the Christians at Ephesus to live holy lives, drawing attention to this positive aspect: 'Let him that stole steal no more: but rather let him labour, working with his hands the thing which is good, that he may have to give to him that needeth' *(Ephesians 4.28)*. Let us endeavour to be honest, industrious people, who are able to give to those in need from that which we have earned.

(1) Our Possession

The Christian should be very conscious that all he has is due to the mercy of God. In *Psalm 24.1*, we are reminded that everything belongs to God: 'The earth is the Lord's, and the fulness thereof.' Nevertheless, there can be a great difference between one man's possessions and another. It is very important to have a right attitude to what we possess. *Hebrews 13.5* gives us this instruction: 'Be content with such things as ye have.' Are we content with what we have – health, wealth, family, friends, situation, circumstances? When our priorities are right and we appreciate the riches that we have in Christ, then our correct attitude to material things becomes apparent. The apostle Paul, in *Philippians 4.11*, tells us what he has learned with regard to worldly goods: 'For I have learned, in whatsoever state I am, therewith to be content.' He was in prison when he wrote these words, and had nothing apart from the clothes in which he stood and the chains that held him.

Some believers will be rich in the things of this world and some will not, but all must find their contentment in godliness and in the pursuit of righteousness. The poor must beware that the seed or root of bitterness does not take hold in their hearts; this can be the beginning of trouble. The rich also can fall into a snare: the rich man can so easily delight in his possessions and begin to desire more. In the Scriptures, we have an illustration of the danger of prosperity in the life of King David. As we have read in the previous chapter, he had plenty and yet he looked upon the wife of another man. David had many wives, but this woman was Uriah's only wife. David saw to it that Uriah had the greatest privilege that a man could have: to die for his king. He put him in the front line of the battle where he was guaranteed to be killed, and David was legally able to take Uriah's wife. Later, the prophet Nathan came to David and told him of a certain man who had many, many sheep; one day a guest came by, so the rich man decided to kill a lamb in order to provide a feast for that guest. There was a poor man who lived on the borders of his land who had just one lamb. This lamb was taken and killed in order to provide his guest with food. David was furious when he heard this account and said, 'That man should be brought to judgement. It is terrible that such a rich man should take from a poor man who has so little.' The prophet replied, 'Thou art the man.' It went home to David and in *Psalm 51.1-3*, he pours his heart out in sorrow before the Lord: 'Have mercy upon me, O God, ... for I acknowledge my transgressions: and my sin is ever before me.'

We may well wonder: how is it possible for a Christian to be a thief? The Christian can be a thief in a number of ways. David found himself stealing. Today, stealing is so commonplace that Christians can find themselves stealing without realising. The Bible tells us that all stealing is wrong.

In the book of *Malachi 3.8*, we find a form of stealing that the Christian can very easily fall into: 'Will a man rob God? Yet ye have robbed me. But ye say, Wherein have we robbed thee? In tithes and offerings.' How easily we let our tithes slip by and make an offering that can vary according to our mood! Perhaps it is because we have lost sight of the sacrifice of the Lord Jesus Christ on Calvary, or that we have never understood anything of what it cost Him, that we will not even give Him a small portion of our time and money. Thank God, our Saviour did not hold back when He received our guilt on the cross. We, however, can be respectable thieves, holding back that which belongs to the Lord. We are reminded, in the words of this verse, that, ultimately, nothing belongs to us:

> *All that I am, He made me.*
> *All that I have, He gave me.*
> *All that I ever hope to be,*
> *Jesus alone can do for me.*

The Christian must learn the right attitude towards material things. Our homes, our property, our time and our interests belong to the Lord. We must be conscious that we, too, are the Lord's, that our life is not our own and that we have been bought with a price. When George Matheson penned the following lines, he had already come to the place where he realised that his life was not his own:

> *O Love, that wilt not let me go,*
> *I rest my weary soul in Thee;*
> *I give Thee back the life I owe,*
> *That in Thine ocean depths its flow*
> *May richer, fuller be.*

1 Timothy 6.6 goes even further: 'But godliness with contentment is great gain.' Do we consider godliness and contentment to be great gain? Whether we have an abundance of this world's goods or whether we possess very little, if we are Christians, we must all find our contentment in godliness and in the pursuit of righteousness.

(2) Our Provision

To safeguard any possibility of our robbing God of that which belongs to Him, we must be aware of the Lord as the great and faithful Provider. It is a wonderful thing to believe in the absolute sovereignty of God; that He is supreme in the great and the small things in our lives. We must concentrate on the Giver, knowing that He knows our need, what is good for us and what He can trust us with. This can be seen in two ways. Can He trust us to be poor and still have a correct attitude? Can He trust us to be rich and still maintain a right attitude of heart? What should our priority be? It should always be one of seeking God Himself and His will: 'But seek ye first the kingdom of God, and his righteousness; and all these things shall be added unto you' *(Matthew 6.33)*.

There are times when we are tested and we wonder, 'Will His hand provide for us?' How many volumes could be written about God's amazing ways and His perfect timing? How often has He intervened and helped us when all seemed against us? We must never lose faith in God to provide for all our needs, as we are precious in His sight. In *Matthew 6.28-29*, we are given an example of God's care for us: 'And why take ye thought for raiment? Consider the lilies of the field, how they grow; they toil not, neither do they spin: and yet I say unto you, That even Solomon in all his glory was not arrayed like one of these.' If God has such concern for detail, He certainly is not unmindful of the needs of His children. We must never fear when such a God, who is fully aware of all our needs, is ours. Such care can be seen in the words of the Saviour, in the following verses in *Matthew 6.30-32*: 'Wherefore, if God so clothe the grass of the field, which to day is, and to morrow is cast into the oven, shall he not much more clothe you, O ye of little faith? Therefore take no thought, saying, What shall we eat? or, What shall we drink? or, Wherewithal shall we be clothed? (For after all these things do the Gentiles seek:) for your heavenly Father knoweth that ye have need of all these things.'

To be filled with such questionings and anxieties will only lead us more and more into the fields of discontent and greed. This is no place for the Christian, for here he rapidly loses sight of the hand of God and the assurance in his heart that God will take care of him. We must keep a constant watch upon our hearts to safeguard this relationship and maintain this implicit trust in God. Listen to the words of our Saviour in *Matthew 6.34*: 'Take therefore no thought for the morrow: for the morrow shall take thought for the things of itself. Sufficient unto the day is the evil thereof.'

If we are rich today, we may be poor tomorrow and if we are poor today, we may be rich tomorrow. Whatever we may be today or tomorrow, if we have our principles right, our attitudes to wealth and possessions will not change. Our times are in His hands. In poverty and wealth, in sickness and in health, in a promised long life, or days that are numbered, do we really believe that the Lord is our Shepherd, and that we shall not want?

True Christianity is a deep, a spiritual and a beautiful thing. It is more lovely than a lily. We are saved by richer grace and washed in nobler blood than has flowed in any veins. We will have a right view of our possessions, because we know that we have a right view of our provisions. God will provide what is good for us, and in this place of trust, we will not steal.

(3) Our Position

When the Lord Jesus Christ died on Calvary, He died between two thieves, yet He was no thief. Even there on the cross, the miracle of making one of them an honest man was made possible because of His death that is the penalty for our sin. The Lord is the example of absolute honesty and integrity. He has purchased our salvation for us. We cannot buy salvation, we cannot steal it, we cannot get it by any other way than by the grace of God through Christ. A hymn by William Cowper, which includes this verse, places the dying thief, who represents us all, at the foot of the cross:

> *The dying thief rejoiced to see*
> *That fountain in his day;*
> *And there have I, though vile as he,*
> *Washed all my sins away.*

What a wonderful sight! There He is. He is not a thief, yet as a thief He dies. Not a murderer, yet as a murderer He dies. Not an adulterer, yet as an adulterer He dies, with no dishonour and yet without honour, dying for you and for me and making us clean. It is an amazing thing that when we come to Him as converts we are made new; by keeping near to Him, our radiance, and indeed our transparency, can be maintained. We become people without guile who are honest in thought, word and deed. This is a great miracle and can only come about as the result of a work of grace in our hearts. May we always strive to be a pure and delightful people, and steal none of the glory for ourselves, being content with such things as we have.

The Law of Love

Chapter Nine

Thou shalt not bear
false witness against
thy neighbour.
Exodus 20.16

What a terrible thing it is to be false, yet it takes spiritual self-discipline to be true! People can so readily hide their mistakes with a lie, to avoid immediate embarrassment. To be false ultimately makes it very difficult for anyone to live with himself. Eventually every shred of self-respect has disappeared. The opposite is particularly beautiful when we think of a person who is without guile, and does not, and will not, participate in anything that is devious.

What a test it must have been for the Lord Jesus Christ when faced with false accusations! How easy it would have been for Him to have become angry, but He neither threatened nor reacted. Undoubtedly, He would have felt great compassion for the terrible state of heart of His accusers. They were to be pitied, although they could not be excused for their behaviour. In *Mark 14.55-58*, we read the detailed account of how the people tried to bring accusations against Him: 'And the chief priests and all the council sought for witness against Jesus to put him to death; and found none. For many bare false witness against him, but their witness agreed not together. And there arose certain, and bare false witness against him, saying, We heard him say, I will destroy this temple that is made with hands, and within three days I will build another made without hands.' Here we have the prime example of bearing false witness and, at the same time, the gentle and gracious attitude of our Lord. The most dangerous kind of false witness is when it contains an element of truth: someone can bring an accusation against another person that has some truth in it which makes it appear credible, yet it misrepresents that person. Such a lie is very dangerous.

When our Lord spoke these words, He was not speaking of the actual temple. He spoke of the temple of His body, and of His death and resurrection, but they deliberately chose to misunderstand His words and use them as a testimony against Him. To this, He said nothing. He held His peace. We behold the scene recorded for us in Scripture and we feel like saying, 'They are not telling the truth. They are being grossly unfair in the way they regard the person of our blessed Saviour, the Lord Jesus Christ.' Yet He remained silent and did not defend Himself. Those men who opposed Christ were determined to crucify Him.

Sometimes we can be determined not to receive anything from the Word of God; we can be determined to be hearers only and not doers of the Word. We are so ready to cover our tracks with an untruth. There is much that we can learn from the simplicity that is in Christ when He told us that our 'yes' should be 'yes' and our 'no' should be 'no'. We cannot follow this second section of the commandments, in loving our neighbour, if we allow a false spirit to dwell within us.

(1) The Word That Wounds

When James was writing his epistle it was, and still is, very forthright. It is an alarming thing to consider that he is addressing Christians: 'Out of the same mouth proceedeth blessing and cursing. My brethren, these things ought not so to be' *(James 3.10)*. The same mouth, the same person, can be responsible for this double-talk. 'A double minded man is unstable in all his ways' *(James 1.8)*. Are we double minded? Are we two-faced? These are the questions we must ask ourselves. Are we able to say to someone who calls unexpectedly that we are really glad to see them, but immediately the front door closes, we say, 'Did they have to call?' This is the kind of thing that we are talking about: double mindedness, two-facedness. To control this behaviour, as Christians, we must ask for grace. Such behaviour is a contradiction to the term 'Christian'. We cannot have the same tongue both blessing and cursing at the same time. It should not be so. We must search our hearts and consider our attitudes. James goes on to question how much grace there can really be in that person's heart by asking: 'Doth a fountain send forth at the same place sweet water and bitter? Can the fig tree, my brethren, bear olive berries? either a vine, figs? so can no fountain both yield salt water and fresh' *(James 3.11-12)*.

This kind of behaviour brings into doubt a person's spiritual state, and whether they are progressing in the ways of God at all. It should be impossible for the Christian, who has a fount of grace within his heart, to behave in such a way: to curse and to bless at the same time; to speak sweet words with his mouth and to have bitterness in his heart; to say one thing openly and then in his heart to feel very differently indeed. We must be people without guile.

There are so many ways of bearing false witness. There is the obvious lie and misrepresentation, as well as the subtle suggestion of doubt. It is the latter that I find particularly damaging. The former is obvious and clumsy and there is no doubt in anyone's mind what is happening, but the clever, undermining word can destroy another person. We can do it in a detached way: 'He's a very nice person, you know, he's very good and enthusiastic, and he's very sincere … er … but you know, he goes … er … too far, he's … er … like this, like that.' To cast doubt upon anybody is wicked; to cast doubt upon a brother in Christ will hold us answerable in the day of Christ.

Planting a seed of doubt is like a grain of deadly poison; given time, it will do its deadly work. We may not murder, but we can be guilty of character assassination and kill another person's spirit with our words. James reminds us how dangerous the tongue can be: 'Even so the tongue is a little member, and boasteth great things. Behold, how great a matter a little fire kindleth!' *(James 3.5)*. It has often been said that a lie flames more quickly than truth. I sometimes think that it exceeds the speed of light! That is why I say it is a wicked thing and one for which we will be answerable in the day of Christ. We must be careful of our words, for words wound deeply. We could destroy one another so easily. We must remember that there is the more excellent way of love.

(2) The Word That Weighs

The damage caused by a lie cannot be measured. James gives full expression to the extent of damage that the tongue can cause in *James 3.6*: 'And the tongue is a fire, a world of iniquity: so is the tongue among our members, that it defileth the whole body, and setteth on fire the course of nature; and it is set on fire of hell.' Hell is eternal and these evil things are born of hell. When the Christian behaves in this way, he is allowing devilish things to take over in a place where grace should reign. Does grace reign in our tongue? Does grace reign in what we say? Are we careful of our words? How important our words are! The power of hell is let loose as Satan, named by our Lord Jesus Christ as the father of lies, is closely involved with all that is treacherous and evil. What does all this do to the individual? He becomes a liar!

Our words weigh us up and show us for what we are. In many ways, the words of a man are the mouthpiece of his heart. Sooner or later, he will express himself and display what lies in his heart. This is what is meant by these words in *Matthew 12.35-37*, spoken by Christ to the Pharisees: 'A good man out of the good treasure of the heart bringeth forth good things: and an evil man out of the evil treasure bringeth forth evil things. But I say unto you, That every idle word that men shall speak, they shall give account thereof in the day of judgement. For by thy words thou shall be justified, and by thy words thou shalt be condemned.'

In the courts of the world, perjury is looked upon with great seriousness. One lie can cause a man to be condemned and sentenced. The whole course of a case can be determined by one witness. To give false witness is a dreadful thing; to be a false witness is tragic. I can almost hear many say that they would never be that kind of a person, but God knows our hearts. These warnings would not be in His Word unless He knew well the subtle ways that the flesh wars against the spiritual man. We can speak freely, but we must be careful that they are neither idle words, nor wounding or false-witnessing words. We are answerable for our words, even though we may be sorry for many things that we have said. They will still have their rebuke or reward in the day of Christ.

What will it be like when we stand before the great God Himself, in all His holiness, when we have committed perjury? What will it be like when a man of grace has allowed his tongue to kindle a fire that burns up the character of someone else and has allowed his tongue to blacken the character of another for his own advantage, or to hide his own sin? We shall not be lost, if we are the Lord's, but we shall be weighed and rebuked. We are new creatures in Christ; let us be without guile.

(3) The Word That Wins

How can we be such men of grace without the grace of God? Sometimes we may feel that we are impossible cases and that we can never be anything approaching that which is well-pleasing in His sight. Yet a work of grace has begun and God is able to see it through. But what shall we do with this unruly tongue that James speaks of, in *James 3.8*? 'But the tongue can no man tame; it is an unruly evil, full of deadly poison.' Grace is able to control the tongue, and the speaker's heart. James gives examples of how grace can work: it is like a bit placed in the most tender part of a horse's mouth to guide his direction and it is also like a rudder which can rule the course of a great ship, pointing it in the direction it must go. In a similar way, the tongue can utter words of great influence that can have deep and lasting effects for good or evil.

We must then see to it that our words are from an honest heart. Let us learn to seek out opportunities to encourage and to help one another. What a difference a kind word makes to a sad heart as we pass by! What a tremendous influence the truth has when we speak in a world of lies! Consider then the words of grace that tell men and women of the unsearchable riches of Christ. These are words that win the hearts of men and women. These are words of grace that bring great victory to a kingdom that loves truth.

Are we willing to go that far? Are we willing to tell the truth about Christ, about His gospel of salvation? Are we willing *not* to tone down the Gospel? Are we willing not to alter it in any way? We must not pervert the Gospel so that it no longer looks anything like the truth that men spoke of, so honestly, in those early days. Let us not be false witnesses but let us be true. Let us honour His truth that we might be well-pleasing in His sight. If we find it difficult, He will give us grace.

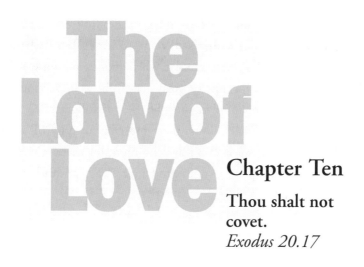

The Law of Love

Chapter Ten

Thou shalt not covet.
Exodus 20.17

Thou shalt not covet thy neighbour's house, thou shalt not covet thy neighbour's wife, nor his manservant, nor his maidservant, nor his ox, nor his ass, nor any thing that is thy neighbour's *(Exodus 20.17)*.

Coveting is a sly sin and can enter into so many parts of our lives. Without saying a word, and keeping a pleasant smile on our faces, we can covet our neighbour's possessions. We may hear a friend receiving praise for a commendable action and we covet the attention. Very easily, envy and jealousy, swiftly leading to anger, can enter our hearts.

When a covetous spirit enters our lives, it is not long before it takes over. Not only are we unwilling to hear of the success and acceptance of another, but a brooding bitterness lays hold of our hearts. Our spiritual life suffers very badly when this happens. It is impossible to enjoy fellowship with the Lord and there is certainly no fellowship with our fellow-believers. Joy has gone, and there is no sign of love and understanding. Without realising, we have become hard, suspecting everyone's motives. There is an old saying which says that a friend in need is a friend indeed. I am sure there is a great deal of truth in that – a little fellow understanding is a very commendable thing. Nevertheless, is it not far more impressive when another person is truly able to rejoice with you in a time of great joy? To be as happy for the joy of another, as if it were our own, must be the work of grace.

If we are to love our neighbours, there must be sincerity of heart and a lovely openness of spirit that leaves no room for these miserable attitudes of covetousness, envy, jealousy and anger. Such a heart is filled with the grace of God.

(1) The Ruin

In Scripture, we are commanded not to: '...covet thy neighbour's wife, nor his manservant, nor his maidservant, nor his ox, nor his ass, nor any thing that is thy neighbour's' *(Exodus 20.17)*. The instruction is a clear one, and goes into detail because there are so many areas of our lives in which we can be covetous. When it happens, it ruins that ability to love our neighbour and spoils the wonderful fellowship that we should have with one another. A question may arise in our hearts, 'How does a person get like this when the grace of God is in his heart?' The answer is that he allows discontent to enter his heart. Discontent can so easily be the ground upon which coveting will thrive. We can look with self-pity upon our lot in any sphere of life, from possessions to abilities, and be discontent. There is a beautiful verse in *Hebrews* that helps us in a very warm way with this particular commandment: 'Let your conversation be without covetousness; and be content with such things as ye have: for he hath said, I will never leave thee, nor forsake thee' *(Hebrews 13.5)*.

What is coveting? We might think that coveting is the mother of stealing, but no, coveting is something quite on its own. They are related but they are not the same. If they were, there would not be a separate commandment. One man said, 'A man who is covetous takes more pain in getting on earth things there, than getting in heaven things there.' It is a good explanation. A covetous person will spend more of the energies of his mind, his thinking, his faculties and his abilities in 'getting on earth'; more time, more energy, more love, more desire than getting things in heaven. This is the malady of our country today. We cannot say that Britain is poverty-stricken, but was there ever a time when people wanted more? We look at our troubled land, our unregenerate nation, and we can say that there is a malady of covetousness. Where once man used to have to fight for his very existence, today he is intent on getting gain in a way that is almost malicious. One wonders where the end of it all will be. There is no satisfaction. As an illustration, let us take an illness like cancer which can lie hidden for a long time. It has many and varied symptoms and forms, and it is only in the later stages that it shows its ugly effects. Covetousness is like that.

The apostle Paul describes it as a cloak, in *1 Thessalonians 2.5*: 'For neither at any time used we flattering words, as ye know, nor a cloke of covetousness...' Why does Paul liken it to a cloak? A cloak is something that can hide or disguise what lies beneath it. Likewise, covetousness has many disguises. It can come amongst God's people saying, 'Look, everyone is well-off today. Take care of your own affairs; it is what everybody else is doing, so you do the same.' 'If you work on the Sabbath, you get double pay; other people are getting more, why shouldn't you?' 'Why shouldn't you have these material things? Everyone else has them; you can make it up in some other way for not being in church on the Sabbath day.' As an aside, I should mention that we are not referring to deeds of mercy and deeds of necessity. Here is another way that covetousness can come upon us: we can think ahead to the future, to a time when we will not be able to look after ourselves, and so we provide for our future far more than is necessary. It is a cloak of covetousness.

Each one of us must examine our hearts to see if we have a cloak of covetousness. We can say that we have been saving and are being careful, and yet we know that we have more than we could ever want.

Someone once said, 'For one man, when he has £100, he is rich; for another man, when he has £10,000, he says that he is poor.' We fail to examine ourselves as we should, and often find that those who have the most, are more concerned about their money than those who have none. The more we have, the more we hold on to it. The more we have, the more we want. The more we have, the more afraid we are that we will lose it. It is a cloak of covetousness.

What does covetousness do to us? It is dangerous in the spiritual realm because it checks the work of grace. It is an enemy to God's work of grace in our hearts. It can choke the missionary work of the church. It can choke the outreach of the church. It can choke our own giving. It can choke our attitude to money matters, possessions and time. We will only give so much of our money. We will only give so much of our possessions. We will only give so much of our time, and then we find ourselves dictating to God. He just says simply to us, 'Thou shalt not covet.' Is it not true that we would have nothing, not even the breath in our bodies, were it not for the mercy of God? He could take all from us now.

It has been said of the Christians who once escaped from East Germany to the West, that they wished to return. They did not want to return because they loved persecution, but because they saw the damage caused by materialism in the 'free world'. Materialism had damaged the Christians in the West more than persecution had damaged the Christians in East Germany. Those Christians preferred persecution to materialism. They did not want to become what we in the West had become.

Covetousness is a thief. It is a thief in the arena of God's grace. It has devastating consequences. It is invisible. If a person has little, he can still be covetous. He can desire what the rich man has. He may have no talent and may desire the talent of the man who has much. Covetousness is not restricted to the area of money. We can look at another's health, youth, vigour, strength or a wide spectrum of things, and covet. We can look slyly at the next person and say, 'I wish I were as strong as him.' 'Why should he be healthy?' 'Why should he have that?' Desires like these destroy the fellowship of the church. They are like bindweed, the most terrible of weeds. It has a very pretty-looking flower when seen amongst the roses. Then we begin to see what is happening to the rose bush. Examining the bindweed, we see that it has such a slender and weak little stem, but have we really looked at it? It wraps itself around the rose bush to such an extent that it takes all our strength to tear it away. When we do tear it away and look at all the damage it has done to the plant, we are amazed. We try to get at its roots and find that the stems will easily snap, but it will keep its roots. We have to dig deep in order to get rid of the roots of a bindweed. Covetousness is like that – it chokes. It will bring wrong attitudes toward our fellow-believers who may be gifted or rich. It will even bring wrong attitudes towards our fellow believers who may be gracious, with a right attitude of heart. It is a disaster course. Self-gain has a very firm grip. When it takes hold of the heart, it takes hold powerfully. The thought of giving, or making any kind of sacrifice, will not even occur to us. We will no longer be aware of the needs of others, because the cry of greed has overwhelmed our hearts with its noisy demands.

(2) The Result

How can we recognise this sin of covetousness if it is always under a cloak? It will always defend self-gain. It will bring a spirit of discontent. It will make us look around at our neighbours and we will find that we no longer love them, even if we sit beside them in the same church. It begins in such a subtle way, by saying, 'Why shouldn't I have a little more?' Covetousness begins in small things. Like the bindweed, we hardly notice it at first; it is so little in the garden. It is hardly worth picking up compared to the dandelions and the daisies that grow by the score. The dandelions and daisies are harmless compared to this. They do not kill other plants in the way that bindweed does. The bindweed of covetousness strangles and chokes fellowship and it ruins and spoils our relationships with one another.

What then shall we do? Let us heed the words of Paul in the epistle to the *Ephesians 4.30-32*: 'And grieve not the holy Spirit of God, whereby ye are sealed unto the day of redemption. Let all bitterness, and wrath, and anger, and clamour, and evil speaking, be put away from you, with all malice: and be ye kind one to another, tenderhearted, forgiving one another, even as God for Christ's sake hath forgiven you.' A covetous mind can be captured by things that are transient, things that one day we will have to part with. How very sad and foolish it all is! If we were in great pain and someone showed us an object of great beauty in order to capture our interest, it would mean nothing. Pain has clouded the horizon, and the only thing we can think of is some relief from the pain. Similarly, if we were preoccupied with some great sorrow which overwhelmed our thinking, we would show no interest in the things around us. If this is so, how can we set such store on any kind of material gain that can mean so little to us in this life, when we are deprived of the ability to enjoy them? Much more so, in the light of eternity, the passing things of this world must take their humble place. They do not deserve a high place of priority in our thinking. We must be spiritually minded and pursue those things that are spiritual and lay little store on the things we have to eventually leave behind.

(3) The Remedy

We must recognise that covetousness is like a cancer. It needs a very deep therapy treatment. We must recognise that it wears many cloaks, and that it is a deadly thing. How shall we remedy this in our own hearts? Would it not be better if Christians from persecuted countries saw us, not as covetous Christians, but Christians who give generously of all that they have, being glorious examples of godliness? How can we be such people? We begin by trusting God's sovereignty. Are we afraid of trusting Him? The Psalmist, in his old age, was able to testify to God's providential care in his life: 'I have been young, and now am old; yet have I not seen the righteous forsaken, nor his seed begging bread' *(Psalm 37.25)*.

All our satisfaction is in the Lord Jesus Christ. This matter must be settled, once and for all, in our hearts. Who am I? I am a sinner forgiven by God's grace in the Lord Jesus Christ. Where am I going? I am going to heaven where I shall enjoy the peace of God's inheritance forever. How should I live? I should live a life well-pleasing to God by loving Him and loving my neighbour. Can I do this? Yes, by God's grace, I am given enabling grace and can live such a life. Why should I live such a life? Because it is God's will that I should be holy, as He is holy. Again, the epistle to the *Ephesians* provides us with a pattern to follow: 'Be ye therefore followers of God, as dear children; and walk in love, as Christ also hath loved us, and hath given himself for us an offering and a sacrifice to God for a sweetsmelling savour' *(Ephesians 5.1-2)*. We must not be like spoiled children but as dear children, walking in love.

Let us look again at Calvary, at the shed blood, at the horror of that cross. We must look at what He has paid for us and realise that the only worthwhile thing that we have is our salvation. What else can we take with us? With what else can we stand before God? What other argument can we have, other than we are saved by grace, and by grace alone? Let us get to grips with what is expected of a people who have been enlightened by the grace of God. We cannot play around with God. We cannot dismiss His commandments. We are the Lord's and we must walk in His way. What does it matter if we go hungry? What does it matter if we do not have a second suit of clothes? The Scriptures tell us clearly how we should live: 'Set your affection on things above, not on things on the earth' *(Colossians 3.2)*. In *Matthew 6.20-21*, the Saviour addresses His disciples in a similar vein: 'But lay up for yourselves treasures in heaven, where neither moth nor rust doth corrupt, and where thieves do not break through nor steal: for where your treasure is, there will your heart be also.' What is our treasure? What is our heart's delight? As we set our affections on the things that are above, His grace begins to fill our hearts. Our attitudes towards material things change. There is no fuss, no fanfare, but a quiet realisation in our hearts and we cry, 'Oh God, forgive me. Oh God, how could I have become like this? Oh God, help me.'

We are the children of a King, and that King is the King of Kings and the Lord of Lords. Let us, therefore, be a gracious people as He is a God of grace. In the words of this hymn, we find a delightful expression of the law of love and of the kind of Christian heart we should desire to have:

May the mind of Christ my Saviour
Live in me from day to day,
By His love and power controlling
All I do and say.

May the love of Jesus fill me,
As the waters fill the sea;
Him exalting, self abasing,
This is victory.

May the Word of God dwell richly
In my heart from hour to hour,
So that all may see I triumph
Only through His power.

May I run the race before me,
Strong and brave to face the foe,
Looking only unto Jesus
As I onward go.

May the peace of God my Father
Rule my life in everything,
That I may be calm to comfort
Sick and sorrowing.

May His beauty rest upon me
As I seek the lost to win,
And may they forget the channel,
Seeing only Him.

Katie Barclay Wilkinson